CATHOLIC POWER
VS.
AMERICAN FREEDOM

GEORGE LA PIANA

CATHOLIC POWER
VS.
AMERICAN FREEDOM

GEORGE LA PIANA & JOHN W. SWOMLEY
EDITED BY HERBERT F. VETTER

 Prometheus Books

59 John Glenn Drive
Amherst, New York 14228-2197

Published 2002 by Prometheus Books

Inquiries should be addressed to
Prometheus Books
59 John Glenn Drive
Amherst, New York 14228–2197
VOICE: 716–691–0133, ext. 207
FAX: 716–564–2711
WWW.PROMETHEUSBOOKS.COM

06 05 04 03 02   5 4 3 2 1

Library of Congress Cataloging-in-Publication Data

La Piana, George, 1879–1971.
    Catholic power vs. American freedom / George La Piana and John M. Swomley ; edited by Herbert F. Vetter.
        p. cm.
    Includes bibliographical references and index.
    ISBN 1–57392–848–8 (alk. paper)
    1. Catholic Church—United States. 2. Democracy—Religious aspects—Catholic Church. 3. Catholic Church—Controversial literature. 4. Church and state—Catholic Church. 5. Church and state—United States. I. Title: Catholic power versus American freedom. II. Swomley, John M., 1915– III. Vetter, Herbert F., 1923– IV. Title.

BX1407.D45 L3 2002
282'.73—dc21

2002069816

Printed in the United States of America on acid-free paper

CONTENTS

PART TWO: AN AFTERWORD
TO GEORGE LA PIANA
by John M. Swomley

PREFACE

George La Piana, a priest-scholar and member of the Modernist movement, which sought the reform of the Roman Catholic Church, wrote *A Totalitarian Church in a Democratic State: The American Experience* in 1949. Born in Italy in 1878, La Piana first considered careers in law, politics, or the history of art, but at twenty-two was ordained a Roman Catholic priest. After teaching from 1900 to 1913 in the Theological School of the University of Palermo and serving as the Rector of San Rocco College, La Piana migrated to the United States, joining his three brothers in Milwaukee, Wisconsin, where he hoped to obtain a position at Marquette University, but the Milwaukee archdiocese hesitated to recommend him. So he joined his brothers in their work, serving as editor of their fortnightly newspaper.

One day when he and his sister were out walking before supper, he was in civilian clothes when they met Monsignor P. M. Abbelen, who angrily accused him of "typical Italian deviltry." Then, without the young priest's having any opportunity to explain that this young woman was his sister, the chancery suspended La Piana's right to say mass.

At the suggestion of a Unitarian minister in Milwaukee, Dr. La Piana undertook a sociological survey of the Italians in Milwaukee, not failing to note the discord among the Irish, German, and Polish communities with respect to control of the Roman Catholic hierarchy. The minister, the Rev. Lyman Greenman, introduced La Piana to the Harvard Divinity School, and he received a fellowship to the school in 1915, and then taught there from 1916 until his retirement in 1947 as the John H. Morison Professor of Church History.

George La Piana became a naturalized citizen of the United States in 1918. In the late 1920s, this ardent anti-Fascist wrote discerning articles for *Foreign Affairs* and *The Nation*. In 1929 he publicly opposed the treaty between Pope Pius X and Benito Mussolini, two powers he considered totalitarian. Dr. La Piana's research clearly included far more than early and medieval Christianity. He described "The First Ten Years of Fascism" and "The Vatican and Fascism." With Professor Gaetano Salvemini, he coauthored, in 1943, a book entitled *What to Do with Italy?* La Piana and Salvemini emphasized the importance of the establishment of democracy in Italy and advocated the separation of church and state. Dr. La Piana was, in fact, consulted on church-state issues by U.S. Supreme Court Justice Felix Frankfurter. Likewise, he served as a consultant to Paul Blanshard, author of a Beacon Press sequence of volumes on church-state relations, beginning, in 1948, with *American Freedom and Catholic Power*. Blanshard was committed to concealing the fact that his expert adviser was La Piana, since the historian feared that the Vatican might excommunicate La Piana, just as it had excommunicated his Modernist friend, Ernesto Buonnaiuti.

In 1949, after retirement from Harvard, Dr. La Piana delivered a series of four lectures titled *A Totalitarian Church in a Democratic State* at Butler University in Indianapolis, Indiana. Blanshard wrote the following words in a previously unpublished letter dated August 7, 1949, now in the La Piana archives of the Andover-Harvard Theological Library, Harvard University (George La Piana Papers bMS 104):

> I have just finished reading your brilliant and interesting lectures at Butler. I do hope that they can be embodied as the core of a book on the history of the Catholic Church in the United States. Your scholarly knowledge in this field makes you the logical person to undertake the work, and the interest in the subject is now so immense that it should be easy to find a publisher.
>
> I suppose you know about the rather astonishing success of my book (*American Freedom and Catholic Power*). Beacon Press is planning a SIXTH printing next week, bringing the total to 40,000. The book sold 2,500 copies last week alone, thanks to the [Cardinal] Spellman–[Eleanor] Roosevelt controversy. *Prof. [Horace]

---

*Eleanor Roosevelt wrote in a June 1949 "My Day" syndicated newspaper column that parochial schools are fine for people who choose them, but they should receive no public tax support. In response, New York City Cardinal Francis Joseph Spellman publicly declared that he would never again publicly acknowledge her since her act of discrimination was unworthy of an American mother.–ed.

Kallen effectively referred in his *Saturday Review* notice to your part in helping to make the book foolproof. In all the attacks on it, no serious errors have been disclosed.

Dr. La Piana's Butler lectures were published in the *Shane Quarterly* (April 1949), a journal of the university's School of Religion, but they were never published as a book. When I visited him in 1960 at his home in Wellesley Hills, Massachusetts, he gave me a personally marked copy of his lectures with the hope that they might at last be published as a book. He died on his ninety-third birthday, February 28, 1971. At St. Paul Roman Catholic Church in Cambridge, a Requiem High Mass was held in celebration of his life. Now the Butler University lectures continue to pose, to Catholics and non-Catholics alike, an insistent question: *To what extent is Roman Catholic authoritarianism a threat to democracy in the United States?*

To sharpen the role of La Piana's own answer to this question, here is a photocopy of a letter written to Professor La Piana by Justice Felix Frankfurter of the United States Supreme Court from 1939–62:

Supreme Court of the United States
Washington 15. D. C.

CHAMBERS OF
STICE FELIX FRANKFURTER

My dear George La Piana:

Long before the illumination which you gave me through your Butler Lectures, you were my unofficial theological adviser, and since gratitude is the expectation of lively favors to come I turn once more to you - as a form of gratitude, in the manner of speaking, for your past intellectual beneficence.

This time I want from you a bibliography - authoritative of course but within the compass both of time and the understanding of a busy judge - on the concept of "sacrilegious" as it has come down through the ages in the Church of Rome. Specifically I am particularly interested in discussions, if there be any, showing the changes in that concept from time to time and indeed contemporaneous conflicts. Perhaps I better tell you the assumption on which I am turning to you for aid. If it is wrong, throw this letter in the wastebasket. It is that the concept of sacrilegious is not fixed, final and definite, but has its own history of changes and chances, of diversities and distinctions, of conflicts and controversies. (I hope you will not infer from this that I have reached that stage of senile juvenility where one again indulges in the youthful excesses of alliteration.)

And please do not send a semi-educated judge references to Greek and Latin texts. Even in Washington there are only twenty-four hours a day, apart from my linguistic illiteracy. When counsel from time to time tell me there are twenty authorities for a proposition I tell them one first-rate, or two or three, is enough.

I hope the world goes well with you. I know it goes better since Salvemini's return. Give him my love and take some for yourself.

Faithfully yours,

Felix Frankfurter

Professor George La Piana.

(George La Piana Papers, bMS 104, Andover-Harvard Theological Library of Harvard University)

La Piana's study reaches from early Christianity to the middle of the twentieth century. At the advent of the twenty-first century, has the situation changed so significantly? In response to this question, I invited an update of the religious situation in the United States by John Swomley, a political scientist who has spent his life as an international exemplar and teacher of Christian social ethics. He served for many years as a member, as well as vice president, of the national board of the American Civil Liberties Union and chaired the Church-State Committee of the ACLU for many years.

Swomley lives on the boundary of critical thought and decisive social action. One early symbol of his effective national power was his persistent and strategic eight-year leadership of the battle which led to the vote by Congress after World War II not to establish Universal Military Service for every male in the United States. He has had a continuing commitment to nonviolent direct action throughout the civil rights movement, including helping to foster the liberating deeds of Martin Luther King. Lively details about his life are available in his two latest books: *Confronting Church and State: Memoirs of an Activist,* and *Confronting Systems of Violence: Memoirs of a Peace Activist.*

In addition to many decades of aggressive peacemaking, Swomley has done substantial written work. His writings include hundreds of articles in periodicals such as *The Nation,* the *Christian Century,* the *National Catholic Reporter, Religion and Education,* and the *Journal of Law and Religion.* Among his books are *Religion, the State, and the Schools; American Empire; Liberation Ethics;* and *Religious Liberty and the Secular State.*

When I requested the Swomley manuscript—his updating of the bold La Piana historical thesis—he completed this task as his top priority while he was suffering from life-threatening cancer, which is now in full remission. Week after week he would send me a single chapter, never knowing if he would live to send another.

For assistance with this book, I wish first to thank two colleagues who studied with La Piana and who shared their memories of their experience: Max Gaebler, who long served as minister of the First Unitarian Society of Madison, Wisconsin; and Jack Mendelsohn, whose ministry has included the Arlington Street Church, Boston, and the First Unitarian Church of Chicago.

I am also grateful to the late Dr. George H. Williams, La Piana's distinguished successor at Harvard, both for personal conversations and and also for his definitive article published in the April 1973 issue of the *Harvard Library Bulletin*: "Professor George La Piana (1878–1971), Catholic Modernist at Harvard (1915–1947)."

Thanks also to Jeannette Hopkins, my consultant and friend, now retired as director of the Wesleyan University Press; to Thomas Ferrick, a colleague, a former Roman Catholic priest, and now the Humanist Chaplain at Harvard; and to Edd Doerr, executive director of Americans for Religious Liberty, for his help in perfecting this manuscript. Appreciation is due to Veronica Jung, who helped substantially to make this an intelligible manuscript able to evoke dialogue.

I thank, above all, my wife Dorothy, a true partner for fifty years.

Herbert F. Vetter
Cambridge, Massachusetts, 2002

PART ONE

A TOTALITARIAN CHURCH IN A DEMOCRATIC STATE

THE AMERICAN EXPERIMENT

BY

GEORGE LA PIANA

1

THE TOTALITARIAN SYSTEM OF MODERN CATHOLICISM

PROTESTANTISM AND TRADITION

In a *Dictionary of Sects, Heresies, Ecclesiastical Parties, and Schools of Religious Thought*, published in London in 1874 by a certain Rev. H. Blunt, the Roman Catholic Church was dismissed with the following definition: "Roman Catholic: a sect originally organized by the Jesuits out of the relics of the Marian party of clergy and laity in the reign of Queen Elizabeth, and further organized into a Donatist hierarchy by Cardinal Nicholas Patrick Stephen Wiseman in 1850." By the same token American Catholicism of today should be described as a sect organized by the Jesuit John Carroll, its first bishop, in 1789, and further organized into a papist church by the Irish bishops who have ruled the American Catholic Church up to this day.

These and similar unhistorical and ludicrous definitions derive from the assumption that only the Protestant churches possess the genuine Christian spirit and tradition, and that Catholicism is a degenerate form of Christianity, a mere sect, a dead branch severed from the mighty old trunk of true Christianity. Contrariwise, Catholic apologists, starting from the premise that only the Catholic Church represents the historical and spiritual continuity of the divine revelation in Christianity, are bound to consider all Protestant churches as a new wild growth barren of fruits, or as broken fragments of Christianity scattered to the four winds.

Modern historiography, which does not start from any a priori theological assumption—not because it denies necessarily the superhuman element in human events, but because this element belongs to the realm of faith and not of history—sees in the history of the Church an organic development of Christian thought and institutions, an evolution of the Christian spirit conditioned by the intellectual, social, economic, and political factors of times and places in history as in life. There is no breach of continuity and, at the same time, there is constant change. From this point of view, modern Catholicism and Protestantism are both living and not dead branches of the same old tree; they have grown out of the same trunk of ancient and medieval Christianity. They have still in common the fundamental notion of redemption through a moral and mystical experience; they both aim at the same final goal, which they still express with the early comprehensive name of Christian salvation. Divergent as their views may be as to the ways and means of reaching the goal, Catholicism and Protestantism, starting from the same premise of a divine intervention in human history, from the same ideas about man and the universe and the same moral and spiritual vision of life, are both witnesses of the inexhaustible vitality of the essential Christian message of salvation.

The assumption that truth is one and indivisible and that this truth is the sacred possession of only one man, or one school, or one religion, or one Church to the exclusion of all others, might be consistent with abstract metaphysical premises, but it has never been and, as far as we can see, it will never be a historical reality. If history has any meaning at all, it should suggest even to theologians that diversity and contrast of ideas and beliefs are part of God's plan as a necessary condition for human progress. Religion and the realm of spiritual experience are no exception; they too fall under the same rule. Uniformity brings stagnation and intolerance, perpetuates myths, and leads to religious totalitarianism. We must not forget that the notion of "chosen people" started with religious connotations and ended in the bloody theory of "racism."

The world has now come to realize as never before that, to save the ideals of civilization from total destruction, what we urgently need is some sort of unity but not uniformity. A unity which recognizes and respects diversity and derives its strength from the willing cooperation of all constructive forces for the common good, a union of nations which should be able to maintain peaceful relations among states and nations of the world, and a union of Christian churches on a common program of religious and social action, is the cherished dream of today. Very little progress has been made toward the realization of this dream. But it has been shown that nationalism and cultural diversity do not inevitably bar the path to a representative organ of unity. It has also been shown that theological differences, important and real as they may be, do not necessarily raise impassable barriers of mutual anathemas. The hope has dawned that the Christian spirit common to all churches may become a stronger bond of union than either dogmas or creeds.

This is not the place to analyze the reasons why these attempts to secure a union, while respecting political and religious diversity, have met with failure. It is obvious, however, that in both cases the main opposition came from the formidable powers which were bent to impose unity by uniformity. The first League of Nations was severely handicapped by the absence in its ranks of the United States, and then received its death blow from the totalitarian states bent on expansion and domination by force. Likewise, the efforts to establish some form of Christian religious union have been greatly handicapped by the absence of the largest Christian denomination, the Roman Catholic Church, which is also, by its own claim, a totalitarian church expecting to conquer the world on the principle that it is the exclusive divine agency of salvation, the exclusive organ of divine grace, and the exclusive channel of the divine spirit.

The Roman Church has rejected all invitations even to discuss the problem of Christian unity with other churches because truth cannot descend from its lofty pedestal and mingle with error, even for the purpose of discussion. If you search after Christian unity, Rome has said, there is only one way of attaining it: Come to Rome, and accept Catholic uniformity within the Catholic authoritarian and totalitarian system. Likewise, the totalitarian regime of Moscow answered the appeal for peace and security of the surrounding nations by annexing them to the Soviet fold, and telling all other nations that peace and security could be established only on Soviet terms. This striking parallelism of claims and policies of a totalitarian state and a totalitarian church is not a casual coincidence. It is the logical conse- quence of their absolute premises which, though they differ one from the other in content and aims, stand in both sys- tems upon the same firm belief that they, and they alone, are right while the others are wrong, and that they, and they alone, have a universal mission entrusted to them either by God or by destiny which must be fulfilled.

The nature and the program of state totalitarianism— this ugly neologism coined in Italy as a comprehensive char- acterization of the Fascist regime—were expressed force- fully in the fascist principle: "Nothing against the state, nothing outside the state." "Nothing against the state" implies the right of the state to forbid and to suppress by force all political nonconformism. Uniformity with no freedom of criticism or opposition to the government is the first fundamental dogma of a totalitarian state. "Nothing outside the state" implies that all aspects of individual and community life, all activities of the citizens be they social, economic, cultural, or even religious, must be brought under the control of the state and be regulated by the state.

Likewise, in totalitarian Catholicism the fundamental rule is "Nothing against the Church, no salvation outside the Church." No tolerance of heretical errors or of disciplinary schisms are theoretically admissible in the Catholic system. By the principle that there is no salvation outside the Church (because the Church, in the person of the bishop of Rome, successor of Peter, holds the keys of Heaven, so that whatever he binds or loosens on earth is bound or loosened in Heaven), the totalitarian power of the Church extends over all aspects of human life. It extends to all actions of people from the beginning of their existence in the womb of their mothers to the grave. Indeed, it extends beyond the grave, in Purgatory, where the Church can hasten the process of expiation; and even in Heaven, where the decrees of the infallible pope are duly registered as divine decrees and where the Church can obtain special favors through the cult and the intercession of the saints.

The totalitarian idea of the state also involves another and more radical principle: this is that the state as such is, in itself and by itself, an ethical entity by definition, which means that the state has, in itself, the moral justification for all its doings, beyond and above all moral rules which may bind the individuals but do not bind the state. Whatever the state does is right, just because the state does it in its own interest and for its own preservation, its growth, and its expansion. The old notion that the state exists for the individuals is reversed; it is the individual that exists for the state.

In the totalitarian church, this notion assumes a higher ethical form, inasmuch as the Church claims to be the exclusive organ of God's moral law. As such, the authority of the Church extends over the whole realm of human actions and institutions; its judgments and decisions on moral matters are infallible and final. The Church is holy; it is assisted perennially by the divine Spirit, and it cannot and does not make mistakes when it lays down the rules of moral conduct for individuals and for the community. These rules have absolute normative power by divine right. Since the supreme end and purpose of life is to reach eternal salvation, and this end can be attained only through the Church, it is right to say that both things are true: The Church exists for the individual, and the individual exists for the Church.

Last but not least, the totalitarian state, assuming the role of representing for either racial or ideological reasons a superior form of civilization, claims the right to expand and to conquer and to impose its rule over other nations. Totalitarian Catholicism, likewise, assuming the role of exclusive agency for the realization of God's plan on earth, claims the right to expand unhindered by any power whatsoever, nay the right to be supported and assisted by the secular powers in the fulfillment of its mission.

It has been suggested that the modern totalitarian state was modeled on the pattern of the totalitarian church. This pattern was followed very closely in the political-administrative organization of the totalitarian state in fascist Italy and then of all other governments of the same type.

The Catholic Church system is based upon the fundamental distinction between the *ecclesia docens*, the Church that teaches, and the *ecclesia discens*, the Church that is taught; that is to say, between the clergy, which alone has the right to teach and to rule, and the laity, which has only the duty to accept without discrimination the whole teaching of the clergy and all the rules and obligations imposed by the clergy. The totalitarian state is likewise based on the fundamental distinction between the political party (the Fascist party, the Nazi party, the Communist party), which alone has the right to impose its ideology and its program of government, and the rest of the people, whose duty is to accept without opposition such ideology and to obey, to fight, and to die for the totalitarian state.

In the Catholic system, the supreme head of government, the pope, is at once the head of the clergy and the ruler of the whole Church, endowed with fullness of absolute powers, not accountable in his administration to anyone, infallible in his teaching so that his decisions are final and there is no appeal from them. Likewise, in the totalitarian state, the supreme head of the government is at the same time the supreme leader of the party, ruling with absolute powers, not responsible to anyone for his administration, and even claiming a degree of infallibility (Mussolini is always right) or a kind of magic inspiration, as Hitler did.

This impressive parallelism of theoretical principles and of institutional features in a totalitarian church and in a totalitarian state should not, however, blind us to the fact that the totalitarianism of the Catholic Church differs essentially from that of the state, because it has a spiritual content and a spiritual purpose which are completely lacking in the latter. In spite of its bureaucracy and the rigidity of its static theology, Roman Catholicism has always kept alive the fundamental traditions of spirituality of the Christian religion. It has always been able to awake and to nourish genuine enthusiasm and unselfish devotion to the ideals of purity and personal sacrifice. Of course, fanaticism and the spirit of domination with its concomitant evils have again and again tainted its religious and social activities. Its stubborn attachment to temporal and political interests has not seldom cast a dark shadow on whole periods of its history. Corruption and decay have at times perverted its institutions. Even so, the Catholic Church has found in itself the inner strength to restore discipline and moral values; it has shown an inexhaustible capacity of external adaptability to new circumstances and new environments, and of changing its technique, yet remaining the same.

The development of the Catholic system of church government can be traced back in its successive historical stages from its beginning in the ancient Church, to the imperialistic universalism of the Middle Ages, and then to the final systematization of Catholic doctrine and the reorganization of ecclesiastical institutions in the modern period, from the Counter Reformation and the Council of Trent, to recent times.

The Christian Church from the early centuries, to keep its identity as the only way of salvation, felt the need of securing a certain degree of doctrinal and disciplinary unity among the Christian communities scattered in the various provinces of the Roman Empire. By the end of the second century, a system of episcopal government was fully developed. Each bishop chosen by the community taught and ruled his church.

This fact that the members of the ecclesiastical hierarchy from the very beginning of the Church were chosen by the community, and that this system of elections was kept for so many centuries and was sanctioned by the famous democratic formula, "*Qui omnibus praeest ab omnibus eligatur*" ("Who is at the head of all must be elected by all"), has given rise to the belief that the original constitution of the Church was democratic and that it was only through a process of degeneration and usurpations that it was turned into a monarchical constitution. This theory is neither entirely right nor entirely wrong. As far as the method of selecting the leaders of the religious community was concerned, namely, their election by the clergy and the people, there can be no doubt that the constitution of the ancient church adopted what we call a democratic procedure. On the other hand, this procedure lacked one of the most essential elements of a democratic constitution, the delegation of powers. The spiritual and charismatic powers of the bishop and of the whole ecclesiastical hierarchy were not delegated to them by the community, for the simple reason that the community did not possess those powers. These powers came from above, from the Holy Spirit which descended upon bishops and presbyters in the act of their ordination through the imposition of hands by other bishops and presbyters standing in the line of succession from those who were believed to have been appointed by the Apostles at the very beginning. The election by the community was thus merely a designation of the person who was to fill the office. From this point of view, the ancient church was not a democracy. If we may call it so, it was a pneumatocracy, the rule of the Spirit. As a matter of fact, the government of the bishop very soon assumed a monarchical form in each church. The emergence in history of the monarchical episcopate was primarily due to the formidable pressure which was brought to bear upon the church by the Gnostic attempt to absorb the Christian theology of redemption and the Christian Church into an eclectic intellectualistic, theurgical, and mythological system which claimed to represent an esoteric doctrinal tradition going back to Jesus himself. The main defense of the Church against this claim was to oppose to it the exoteric doctrinal tradition represented by the identity and the unbroken continuity of the teachings of the bishops who had ruled the churches in succession from the time of the Apostles. As a historian has put it, the *didache* was tied up firmly with the *diadoche*; that is to say, the authenticity of the doctrinal tradition was proved by the apostolic succession of the bishops.

The Christian Church as a whole thus became a federation of Christian communities bound together by the doctrinal and disciplinary agreement of all the bishops. As Cyprian of Carthage said, "*Ecclesia consensus episcoporum*"—the Church is founded on the agreement of the bishops. Unfortunately, however, this consensus episcoporum, this uniformity in the theological interpretations of the Christian revelation and in the discipline of the Church, did not exist and could not be realized by any means in the ancient church. To overcome the disintegrating effects of nonconformist local traditions, the bishops of the oldest and largest churches, which claimed to have been founded personally by one of the apostles, were assumed to possess a more genuine and more authoritative doctrinal and normative tradition than that of the later and smaller churches. Thus the Patriarchs gradually emerged from the episcopal ranks, vested with higher regional authority. When this development, instead of restoring harmony and unity, gave rise to new and more devastating theological conflicts among the great churches, the bishops of Rome, who very early had claimed a unique prominence in the Church and who claimed to be the successors of the two greatest of all apostles, Peter and Paul, supposed to have been joint founders of the Roman Church, asserted their higher authority as representing the only genuine tradition to be accepted as normative by all the churches.

The constitution of the Church was for a long time a combination of these three elements: first, the earlier episcopal government represented by the institution of the general councils, with power to make dogmatic definitions and pass canons and laws for the whole Church. Second, the government of the Church by an oligarchy of bishops gave rise to the system of the great Patriarchates, each having a regional jurisdiction. Third, the monarchial government of the popes went through a gradual development, from a rather indefinite prominence over other bishops to the primacy as judges of final appeal in ecclesiastical conflicts, and finally to the assumption by the pope of the right of universal jurisdiction over the whole Church as Vicar of Christ on earth. Through these successive stages the centralized monarchical constitution of the Catholic Church reached its present form.

In the Middle Ages the papacy also assumed the character, rights, and functions of a political power and fought with excommunications, as well as with more effective weapons in the battlefields, to maintain and extend its temporal domains and impose its political supremacy and autocratic rule upon emperors and kings. By the end of the fourteenth century, the defeat suffered by the papacy in its conflict with the rising absolute monarchies, and the Avignonese exile followed by the Great Western Schism which rent the Church for over fifty years, marked the collapse of the imperial dreams of the bishops of Rome. The

Council of Constance, which reestablished the union of the Latin Church, also reformed its constitution by going back to the principle of the superior authority of the council above that of the pope, thus restoring the government of the Church by councils to be held every ten years. But the popes restored to their Roman see canceled the decisions of Constance and reaffirmed their divine right to supreme jurisdiction over the universal church.

The Protestant Revolution, which subtracted from the Roman Church a large section of Europe, forced the papacy to finally undertake the work of reforming the Church, *in capite et in membris*, as the phrase went, which had been promised again and again, yet never fulfilled. The Council of Trent, convoked by and kept under the strict control of the pope, issued a series of dogmatic definitions on original sin, justification and redemption, grace, free will, and on the theology of the sacraments, all directed against the teaching of the Protestant reformers. In general, as a reaction against this teaching, the Church went back altogether to the theology of Thomas Aquinas, and it firmly shut the door to any further attempt at new interpretations or new developments in Catholic dogmatics. No less conservative were its decisions concerning the Scripture; the books to be included in the canon; their authorship; their inspiration and their historical, moral, and theological absolute authority. Here again the council tightly closed the door against any attempt to alter the medieval biblical positions. But the most important theological dogma canonized by the council was that which set Tradition on the same level of the Scripture as an instrument of divine revelation. Since Tradition is, on the one hand, the only authoritative guide in the interpretation of the Scripture, and on the other hand, the judge and the main representative of this tradition is the Roman pontiff, the dogmatic definitions of the council virtually implied papal infallibility.

The council also undertook the delicate task of reforming the ecclesiastical institutions, introducing order and uniformity in the administration of the Church, correcting crying abuses and improving the morals of the clergy. The council defined anew the rights and duties and limits of episcopal jurisdiction, issued minute regulations for the appointment to ecclesiastical offices, and above all, it imposed upon all bishops the obligation to establish seminaries—ecclesiastical schools for the training of the clergy under a strict disciplinary supervision. But the council was prevented from making any prescription concerning the reformation of the Roman curia, or the papal court, or anything that touched the pontifical person and the exercise of his authority. This was a task reserved exclusively to the pope himself.

The modern Catholic Church, its dogmatic system and its institutional discipline, are still based on the canons and regulations of the Council of Trent. Since then, there has been in the Catholic Church no further theological development of any major importance, but only the unfolding of all the implications of the doctrine of the monarchical absolutism of the constitution of the Church, which reached its climax in the dogma of papal infallibility of the Vatican Council in 1870, and more recently in the codification of Canon Law. Of this development of Catholic ecclesiology, I shall speak in another connection.

In the field of politics, the papacy continued to be involved in wars and conflicts until the end of the long religious wars which devastated Europe. When the Treaties of Westphalia in 1648 reestablished peace by a compromise, the pope disapproved of it and withdrew his representatives. The papacy ceased to have any influence to speak of on European international affairs. As a political power, it shrunk more and more to the condition of a small territorial sovereignty, subservient to the policies and interests of one or another great European power.

The popes of the seventeenth and eighteenth centuries were on the defensive even in the field of ecclesiastical and spiritual jurisdiction. The Church had tied itself closely to the Catholic absolute monarchies, which recognized the Catholic religion as the religion of the state and refused tolerance to other cults. At the same time, through agreements and concordats, kings and princes had gained control over ecclesiastical institutions, especially over the election of bishops and high ecclesiastical officers, and over the financial resources of the Church. With the rise of the jurisdictionalist theories, the secular power even claimed the right to submit papal decrees and decisions and instructions to the approval of the state before they could be promulgated.

The French Revolution, and then the advent of liberalism and the adoption of free and democratic constitutions by most European states, put an end to the old alliance of the throne and the altar. It is one of the ironies of history that political liberalism, which, on account of its principles of freedom of conscience and religion, was and is still condemned by the Church, was the instrument through which the Catholic Church regained its independence from the state. Political liberalism acknowledged the state's lack of competency in religious matters. Its principles implied not only complete freedom of religion, but also the separation of church and state. The Catholic Church was never reconciled to the regime of religious freedom, and much less to the system of separation. Yet, thanks to the condemned and rejected policies of the liberal secular state, the Catholic Church was able to realize for the first time in its long history the program of a total centralization of all ecclesiastical powers, both spiritual and temporal, in the hands of the papacy. As never before, the whole administration of the Church is now directly controlled by Rome with no interference from the state. All the Catholic bishops are now appointed and removed at will by the pope, and they are responsible for their administration to the pope alone. This gigantic unified system of control has given to the papacy an enormous influence which extends wherever there is an organized Catholic Church. Through the bishops who are bound by a strict oath of fidelity and obedience to the pope, and through the clergy bound by a strict oath of fidelity and obedience to the bishops and to the Holy See, Rome can make its influence felt strongly not only in the religious field, but in the social, economic, and political life of many countries of the world.

It is interesting to notice that in the new system of alliance of church and state, which was established through concordats by the Vatican and the totalitarian states of Italy, Germany, and other nations ruled either openly or in disguise by dictatorial governments, the Church, in order to get a position of privilege over other religions and to get financial support from the state, was willing to grant to the political power, if not the nomination of bishops, as in the old concordats, at least the right to raise objections against any appointment of individuals who were not trusted for political reason by the government. Still more, the bishops elected with the consent of the government had the obligation of taking an oath of allegiance to the state and of denouncing to the authorities any plot or conspiracy against the government which came to their knowledge.

Alliance with the state was always bought by the Catholic Church at a heavy price.

The problem of church and state in the modern world is made more complex for the Catholic Church by the fact that Protestant churches in general have found not only possible, but wholly acceptable, the system of separation and of religious equality before the law. To be sure, Protestantism at its beginning and for a long time afterward believed even more firmly than Catholicism in the alliance of church and state. Being in need of political protection for their very existence, the churches of the Reformation accepted willingly, and even sought, the outright control of the state over their institutions. Catholic historians do not fail to emphasize this point in passing judgment upon the doctrinal and institutional structure of Protestantism.

This judgment was summarized in harsh terms by Pope Pius X in his Encyclical *Editae saepe* (May 26, 1910), published on the occasion of the tercentenary of the canonization of St. Charles Borromeo, one of the leaders of the Counter Reformation. At that time, says the pope, new men came forth whose aim was not the restoration of faith and morals, but rather their deformation and extinction. . . . Under the domination of evil passions, the knowledge of truth was dimmed and disorganized, the struggle against error was fierce and human society, going from bad to worse, seemed to be preparing its own downfall. . . . In the midst of this upheaval proud men and rebels appeared, "enemies of the Cross of Christ yearning after earthly things . . . whose God was their belly." They, having in mind not the correction of morals, but the negation of the fundamental tenets of faith, mixed up everything, opened to themselves and to others a wider path of licentious living, and much more, getting away from the authority and the guidance of the Church and submitting themselves to the yoke of the caprice of most corrupt princes and peoples, tried to destroy the doctrine, the constitution and the discipline of the Church. And then . . . they dared to call this violent rebellion and this onslaught of faith and morals a "restoration," and to call themselves restorers of the ancient discipline. In fact they were corruptors, because having weakened the strength of Europe through conflicts and wars, they hatched the apostasy of modern times, which has brought back the three great evils against which the invincible Church had always stood firm: the bloody battles of her first age, the domestic pest of heresies, and finally that epidemic of vices and destruction of discipline, which under the pretext of safeguarding

the right to a sacred liberty, has spread to a point
which was not even reached in the middle ages.

These words of the pope raised a storm of indignation among German Protestants and caused a diplomatic protest of the German emperor to the Vatican. For the sake of peace, the pope issued a declaration stating that it had not been his intention to offend any special person or institution, and he gave orders to the German bishops not to read the encyclical from the pulpit of their cathedrals, as it was customary to do with such papal documents. But the Italian periodical *Civilta Cattolica* published in Rome by the Jesuits, who may have had a hand in the writing of the encyclical, remarked ironically that some of the sentences which sounded so objectionable to German Protestants had been taken almost verbatim from a page of Martin Luther's own writings against some dissidents in his ranks.

Apart from the harsh words exchanged between Catholic and Protestant controversialists, and in which we must recognize that Luther and other reformers proved to be past masters in the art of vituperation, the views of the Catholic Church concerning the Protestant Revolution and secession have never, and will never, change: Protestantism was and is a heresy; it had its origin in moral corruption because, according to Catholic psychology, the corruption of the heart always precedes the perversion of the mind. In the second place, Protestantism, instead of reforming the morals of the clergy, abolished the law of celibacy, and made a rule of what was an abuse. Moreover, its doctrine of justification by faith alone made unnecessary any moral restraint for the rank and file of the believers. In the third place, Protestantism, far from having gone back to the ancient discipline of the church, broke down the whole disciplinary tradition of the church. Last but not least, by destroying the principle of authority and fostering individualism, Protestantism opened the way to all the evils which afflict modern society. Atheism and anarchism, liberalism and secularism, socialism and communism, fascism and nazism, with all the desolation which they have brought upon the world, are legitimate children or grandchildren of the Protestant Revolution.

This Catholic theological interpretation of history is too simple, to say the least. Unbiased history presents a different and more complex picture of the genesis and the development of Protestantism. It is now obvious that the theology of the reformers was just as medieval as that of Catholicism and was even more rigid in its appraisal of revelation than the intellectualistic theology of Thomas Aquinas. It is true, also, that the reformers were just as intolerant and as ruthless against dissenters as was the Roman Church and its Inquisitors. It is no less true that when they claimed that they were going back to the ancient discipline of the Church, they were victims of an illusion. And finally, it is true that while they set aside tradition as a source of authority and proclaimed the value of individual inner inspiration in the interpretation of the Scripture, they tried to establish at the same time their own tradition and their own interpretation as normative and final for their churches.

But whatever the reformers thought and did, and no matter how archaic and narrow their theology was, or how far they did go in fostering the theocratic principles of monarchical absolutism, or in their attempts to establish a dogmatic dictatorship of their own, the revolution which they started was vital and far-reaching in its implications. They justified their secession from Rome by appealing to the inner light of the spirit, as they had learned from the German mystics, and so they introduced into their reinterpretation of Christianity a dynamic element which had been stifled and obliterated by the crystallization of doctrine into conceptual formulae and by the legalistic institutional overgrowth. Of the two sources of revelation, scripture and tradition, the reformers kept only the former and rejected the latter, but what they really rejected was the static notion of tradition which the theologians had identified with fixed dogmatic creeds and, above all, with the official organs of the government of the Church.

In reality, whether they realized it or not, what the Reformers did was to substitute for a static notion of tradition a dynamic one. They rediscovered that the only path leading to religious life is the experience of the heart and personal decision, and that tradition, that is to say, the transmission of beliefs, of moral principles, and of piety which binds together all Christian generations to the same ideal of Christian life, is effected through the individual and collective spiritual experience in which Christianity lives its most intensive life.

It was this dynamic character of tradition that has enabled Protestantism to submit constantly to new revisions, beliefs, and creeds, and to adopt new forms of institutional organization according to new spiritual and social developments in Christian society. In this development, much of the theology of the reformers has gone overboard, and so have other theological and institutional traditions which had lost their vitality and their efficacy on the Christian spirit.

This is the reason why Protestant churches in modern times—I speak, of course, of those Protestant churches who have overcome the narrow spirit of sixteenth-century reformers—have found not only compatible but in full harmony with their religious beliefs and aspirations, the principles and the practical applications of liberalism and democracy, as well as such modern programs of social and economic reforms which, once they are shorn of their historical connections with positivistic and antireligious premises, could be adopted as reflecting the Christian ideal of real brotherhood and of social justice not merely in words but in action.

The famous French bishop Bossuet condensed his refutation of Protestantism in a single impressive sentence: "Do you change? Then you are in error." To the eloquent bishop change meant breach of continuity, and continuity was identical with immutability. Tradition was a fossilized idol with its eyes turned to the past. One can as well reverse the query and the answer: "You do not change? Then you are in error." As a matter of fact, its claim of immutability notwithstanding, the Catholic Church cannot and has not escaped being affected by the law of development, transition, and evolution inherent in thought and life in all its forms.

Modern Catholicism has totally eliminated from its dogmatic system such remnants of flexibility which it still possessed in the Middle Ages. The return to Scholasticism and to Aquinas imposed by papal decree was supposed to bring back the *philosophia perennis*, the immutable philosophy of all times. It has given rise to several schools of Neoscholasticism in which what is old assumes a pseudomodern form and what is new goes back to Aristotle. As Cardinal Newman remarked, all supposed returns to the past are always innovations.

Very significant is the development on a large scale undergone by the treatise *De Ecclesia* in Catholic theology and Canon Law since the Council of Trent, but especially after the definition of papal infallibility. In the medieval Summae, the treatise on the Church, its nature, its constitution, characters, and prerogatives, was merely an appendix to the treatise on the Incarnation. Today it holds the place of honor at the beginning as a *propedeutica* and starting point of all theological knowledge. It is the portal through which admission is gained to the sacred precinct of Catholic theology.

In the process of expansion of this fundamental subject, the notions of the divine institution and rights, the absolute authority, and the universal jurisdiction and the infallibility of the Roman pontiff are the pivot on which the whole church revolves. Likewise, in the new codification of Canon Law promulgated in 1917, the various sources of law so elaborately described by the old canonists have retained a mere archaeological value and are in fact absorbed into a unique source, the Roman pontiff, who is the authoritative interpreter of divine and natural law, the personification of Tradition and the only supreme and absolute lawgiver for the whole Church. Canonists of today agree that the old notion of *Ius Canonicum* is now superseded by that of *Ius Pontificium*.

To be sure, the medieval theorists of papal autocracy had gone even further by including within the range of pontifical direct jurisdiction the political institutions and powers. But in fact the principle of the ecclesiastical universal jurisdiction of the papacy was in practice limited and coarcted on all sides by local traditions and institutional rights and privileges of national churches, by royal claims and prerogatives, and by the complex entanglements of the ecclesiastical hierarchy with feudal institutions and dynastic overlordships.

Now, on the contrary, all these legalistic chains have been broken and discarded. The most complete centralization of all ecclesiastical powers has been concentrated in the papal bureaucratic organs of universal church administration. Papal absolutism is now, to all purpose, a divine law, intangible forever. All papal decisions, and not only the infallible decrees on faith and morals, induce upon all Catholics a strict obligation to accept them and to obey. "It is necessary," says Pope Leo XIII, "that all Catholics should hold fast with unshakable firmness to all that the Roman Pontiffs have taught or will teach and to make a public profession of it whenever circumstances should require it to do so. Especially in matters concerning the so-called modern liberties, every one must cleave to the judgment of the Apostolic See and act in conformity with its decisions" (Encyclical *Immortale Dei*, November 1, 1885). The totalitarian structure of both the doctrinal and the institutional system of the Catholic Church has thus reached its full expansion and its full height. Solidly anchored on divine law, it defies with confidence all hostile powers.

This Roman totalitarianism does not imply, however, that the government of the universal Church is left in the hands of one man who can do with it whatever he pleases at his whim or caprice. This feature which has been so disastrously characteristic of contemporary dictatorships is ruled out in the modern Catholic Church. The pope, though vested with absolute powers, is the guardian of tradition. Tradition is a vital factor in the theological and institutional life of the Church, and the pontifical power itself rests on tradition. The sense of continuity and immutability, the wide range of divine laws which cover the whole dogmatic and sacramental and such a large part of the institutional system of the Church, the long-standing sacred rules of discipline, and last but not least, the spiritual and moral standards and aims which are essential to the Church for its very existence, are all factors which impose upon its government a fixed rule of teaching and conduct that no pope could challenge without destroying his own power and authority. The institution of the *Ecclesia Catholica* is much greater than the pope himself.

Keeping in mind the characters and the structure of this Catholic totalitarianism of which I have described the most salient features, we must face the serious and complex problem whether and how a totalitarian church can coexist in peace and harmony at the same time and in the same place with a modern democracy.

2

THE CATHOLIC CHURCH, DEMOCRACY, AND RELIGIOUS FREEDOM

T he Christian Church from its beginning was not tolerant toward dissenters in its own ranks. The Church cast them out and consigned them to eternal perdition. At the same time, the Church, persecuted by the Roman government, advocated freedom of religion in the name of the right of each person to worship God according to the dictates of conscience. This contradictory policy of the same Church in the two different cases was suggested by one and the same fundamental principle, the belief that the Christian religion was the only true religion and that the Christian Church was the exclusive divine agency of salvation. As such, the Christian Church denied freedom to dissenters while claiming for itself freedom to exist and to expand unhindered by any human power.

Throughout the centuries of its existence the Christian Church has in general followed this double policy of intolerance for others and freedom for itself. The teaching of Catholic theology on this point is still the same. It may be summarized in three general principles:

1. Condemnation and rejection of freedom of conscience and freedom of religion as theological errors, subversive of all moral principles.
2. Denial in principle of religious tolerance to non-Catholic and non-Christian religions in Catholic countries.
3. Advocation of religious freedom in countries where Catholics form a small minority or where Catholic propaganda is under restrictions or banned altogether.

As we shall see, these normative principles of Catholic policy are submitted to qualifications, limitations, or extensions in the light of other theological and moral principles, as well as of practical needs according to times and places.

First of all, in order to avoid confusion and misunderstanding, it is important to define the meaning of each of these notions, *freedom of conscience*, *freedom of religion*, and *religious tolerance*, which are often employed without discrimination, as if they were more or less equivalent terms.

By *freedom of conscience* we mean the right of every person to choose one's own religion according to the light of reason and the emotions of the heart. Religion is an interior product of conscience through rational conviction and spiritual experience and cannot be imposed from outside.

Freedom of religion means that all religions have an equal right to exist and to be respected and protected by the laws of the state. Religious freedom in this sense is but a corollary of freedom of conscience which the state is bound to respect. In a civilized free state, the practice of freedom of conscience and of religion is limited only by the obligation to respect the accepted moral standards of the community and the exigencies of public order.

Religious tolerance is something different. The notion of tolerance is by definition connected with something which is evil and undesirable. We tolerate things of which we do not approve because we cannot avoid them without incurring a greater evil. Hence Catholic theology admits that the practice of religious tolerance may at times be permitted by the moral law which allows the choice of a lesser evil. Keeping in mind these definitions, we may proceed to the analysis of the Catholic positions and their implications.

The right of a church to expel from its ranks dissenters and rebels cannot be denied in principle. Every society, be it religious or not, has the right to enforce on its members the observance of its statutes. It would be unfair to blame Pope Leo X for not having opened his arms to Luther and clasped him to his bosom. Historians sitting in their armchairs centuries after the events may approve or deplore the narrow dogmatism of churches and their ecclesiastical blunders, or they may speculate about what would have happened if churches had been less intolerant. But as long as church membership is a matter of voluntary choice, and there is no coercion, the internal discipline in religious bodies concerns only the churches and the individuals who join their ranks.

The principle of religious intolerance in Christianity

assumed a social and political aspect only when the Church, under the Christian Roman emperors, began to apply to heretics and rebels the external coercion which was put at its disposal by the state. The first reaction of the great theologians of the fourth and fifth centuries was to deplore and condemn religious coercion. They had seen how such a coercion could be used, as it was used in the Arian controversy, to support orthodoxy against heresy and then, turning the tables, to support heresy against orthodoxy. Above all they knew that a religious faith cannot be imposed by brutal force. "It is the proper character of religion to persuade, not to force" said St. Athanasius. "No one should be compelled to accept our faith by force," said, more energetically, St. Augustine. St. Hilarius of Potier added, "God turns away his eyes in disdain from one who became a Christian by force. God does not need this kind of homage. If force is put at the service of the Church, the Church will refuse this service in the name of its principles."

The principle that faith induced by coercion has no value is part of the Catholic theological tradition, and today it is often emphasized by Catholic clergymen in controversies about religious tolerance. But unfortunately, the practice of the Church did not conform either to the letter or to the spirit of this elementary truth and its implications. Very instructive on this point is the case of St. Augustine (354–430). At the beginning of his ecclesiastical career, he rejected absolutely all forms of coercion in religion: "*Ad fidem nullus est cogendus invitus.*" But later on, confronted with the stubbornness of the Donatists, and having exhausted all the resources of his learning, his zeal and his patience in fruitless attempts to lead them back to the church, he began to think that a measure of coercion, not so extreme as that which the Roman government was then applying to the Donatists, was desirable or even necessary.

Being a conscientious theologian, however, he could not change his mind on this question, or on any other controversial points of theology, without first finding some support in the authority of the Scripture. His older contemporary, John Chrysostom, the great moralist of the Eastern Church, confronted with the same problem of external coercion in religion, had not gone farther than to state that "Our Master certainly does not forbid the repression of heretics and the shutting of their mouth and rejecting their oath." But Augustine wanted something more definite than a mere negative argument. By his inexhaustible ingenuity in biblical exegesis, through the allegorical method, he found the Scriptural authority he wanted, as he usually did find one in support of the doctrines which were dear to his heart. This time it was a parable of the gospel that dispelled his doubts, the parable of the man who invited his friends to a banquet, but all of them, for one reason or another, declined the invitation. Whereupon the indignant host called his servants and bid them to go out in the street, grab the passersby, and force them to enter and to fill the seats around his table: *Compelle intrare*. These strangers, dragged by force to the banquet, in Augustine's interpretation, were the heretics and dissenters who, therefore by this divine command, could and should be compelled to return to the Church.

Having thus justified coercion by the authority of revelation, Augustine and then the theologians in general added other less lofty but more practical reasons, making the recourse to force not only legitimate but indispensable for the good of humanity. The duty of the Church was to protect the weakest members, the simple and ignorant, from heretical infection; the salutary effect of temporal penalties deterring others from falling into the pit of heresy; and last, but not least, the chance that physical suffering might melt the heart of the heretic and finally save his soul. The question was thus settled. Augustine, however, as well as Chrysostom and practically all the ecclesiastical writers for many centuries, opposed the infliction of the penalty of death on heretics. They said that this was forbidden by the gospel and that it violated the sacred principle that *ecclesia abhorret a sanguine*: the Church abhors the shedding of blood.

The history of religious coercion in Christianity, that is, of the coercion which we may call external and physical to distinguish it from the spiritual coercion of the excommunication, has gone through three different successive stages.

The first stage was that of the ancient Church in the Christianized Roman Empire when the Church did not claim to possess any direct external coercive power. This power belonged exclusively to the state, but the ecclesiastical powers expected and demanded that the state should sanction by its laws those of the Church. Thus heresy became a crime also for the state and was punished as such by the secular penal code.

The second stage marked the most fateful step forward made by the Church in the unsavory history of Christian intolerance. In this period the Church claimed to possess and was recognized as possessing direct powers of external coercion apart from and above those of the state. A whole body of ecclesiastical penal legislation was set up by canons of councils and synods and by pontifical decretals. It was administered and applied directly by ecclesiastical courts. The establishment of the universal papal Inquisition in the thirteenth century regularized and introduced more uniformity in the procedure which, by the adoption of physical torture to extract confessions of guilt, was brought up to date with the savage procedure of the secular criminal courts. Heresy continued to be a crime in the concurrent state laws which inflicted the penalty of death by fire to unrepentant heretics or relapsers, handed by the Inquisition to the secular arm. This period in which religious intolerance was severely enforced by both church and state lasted with some slight changes and modifications down to the eighteenth century and in some countries even later.

In the third stage, which covers the nineteenth century to the present, the crime of heresy disappeared from the penal code of the nations which adopted liberal constitutions, and the power of external coercion was denied to the Church. The Catholic Church was left free to excommunicate heretics and rebels and to cast them out of its ranks, but it no longer received any assistance from the state in the enforcement of ecclesiastical sentences of excommunication or of other ecclesiastical penalties. It is this period with which we are primarily concerned.

The social and political conditions of today are neither those of the Middle Ages when the Church was a great political power in its own right, nor those of the period of the absolute monarchies down to the eighteenth century when by the union of church and state, religion, as an *instrumentum regni*, was exploited in support of political absolutism. Political democracy and free political institutions have rejected the union of church and state in favor of the principle of religious freedom. Freedom of conscience and of religion are essential features of modern democracy. In our modern outlook, the establishment of a religion as a religion of the state and the enforcement of its creed or of its laws by the civil government are incompatible with our notion of democracy. Such being the case, it is important to know what is the teaching and the policy of the Catholic Church concerning this modern democracy.

To get a firm grasp of the Catholic position on this point we must turn first to the Catholic doctrine about the Church as a juridical body, as an organization of divine institution. This doctrine may be summarized as follows: The Church is a *societas perfecta*, a perfect society and the only one that is absolutely perfect. The notion of perfect society implies that the Church as a divine institution is absolutely self-sufficient because it is endowed with sovereignty and hence with legislative, executive, and judiciary-coercive powers which are essential to a sovereignty. As such the Church has full and absolute right to employ all the means which in its judgment are necessary or suitable for the fulfillment of its mission. The sovereignty of the Church extends directly over the spiritual realm of life, but indirectly it covers also all temporal things which are in any way connected with the Church and are, therefore, considered as having a spiritual purpose.

The state is a perfect society too, but only in the limited

sphere of temporal things and, from this point of view, the state is subordinated to the Church as the body is subordinated to the soul. The state is thus only relatively perfect. The Church which is absolutely perfect has the right to exercise an indirect power over all other societies to prevent them from raising obstacles to its own activities and to force them to cooperate and to bring their own activities in harmony with those of the Church. The state, therefore, has the negative obligation not to oppose the Church in anything and the positive obligation to supply the Church with material things, means of defense of propaganda, and expansion. Last but not least, the Church by the right of its superior sovereignty has the power to interfere with the legislation and the jurisdiction of the state any time that the state, in the judgment of the ecclesiastical authorities, adopts measures and policies detrimental to the spiritual or moral life of the believers.

As a corollary of these principles of Catholic ecclesiology, the Church condemns as an offense of God's law and a fatal source of evil the separation of church and state and the laws which lower the Church to the condition of a private association existing within the state and as such subject to the general regulations of the state.

It is obvious that a state which should accept these claims of the Church, and should subordinate itself to a higher sovereignty in which it has no part and no control, would cease to be really a sovereign state. The distinction between the direct sovereignty of the Church over spiritual things and only indirect sovereignty over temporal things is for all practical purposes meaningless. Whether their jurisdiction is direct or indirect, it makes no difference in the actual results. Neither does the distinction between the spiritual and the temporal realms, which theoretically assigns to the Church and to the state different fields of sovereignty, solve the problem because the definition of what is spiritual as conceived by the Church includes all temporal things, institutions, and possessions which either belong or are connected with the Church and as such are supposed to have directly or indirectly a spiritual purpose. Last but not least, the universal direct jurisdiction claimed by the Church in the realm of morals in which papal decrees are infallible can be extended to cover all human actions, all institutions, and all aspects of social, economic, and political activities of any community.

As a matter of fact, in the long history of the Church, no state, whatever its form, ever existed, not even in the Middle Ages, which was willing to accept *in toto* these demands of the Church. Whereupon the Church was involved in endless conflicts and was finally forced to make compromises and to accept substantial limitations of its claims. The long list of concordats and agreements made by the papacy with secular rulers throughout several centuries tell the sad story of these compromises. Catholic theologians have now given a systematic form to the principles which bend in practice the rigid theoretical claims of the Church. This is the theory which they call the thesis and the hypothesis. The thesis is the doctrine of the Church which, having its fountainhead in the divine revelation, is eternal, unchangeable, and is not affected by human events or circumstances of times and places. The hypothesis, on the contrary, is the sum total of the circumstances of times and places which make nearly impossible, extremely difficult, or even dangerous, any effort to apply the thesis. In such cases, the Church in making agreements with the state does not insist on the application of the thesis and limits its claims according to the hypothesis. This, however, does not mean that the thesis has been discarded and forgotten. Far from it; the thesis remains intact in its lofty shrine as the goal which should be reached when possible. In other words, the hypothesis implies only a temporary compromise to be set aside in favor of the thesis when circumstances will permit.

It is clear that, as far as the Catholic thesis is concerned, religious freedom and religious tolerance are banned altogether. On the other hand, a modern democratic state that should proscribe these freedoms would cease to be a democracy. On this point the Church and the modern democratic state stand at the opposite poles. No bridge can ever be built over this wide chasm. In the hypothesis, however, the Church makes room for religious tolerance when this appears to be a lesser evil. It is then to the hypothesis that we must turn to find out under what terms it is applied by the Catholic Church.

According to Catholic doctrine, no political regime, no matter what its form may be, which violates the laws of God and of the Church can be considered as being a legitimate form of government. Modern democracy which guarantees to all religious freedom and separation of church and state belongs to this class. This rejection of modern democracy does not mean that the Catholic Church nowadays condemns a priori a democratic constitution of the state in which the government is chosen by the people. Catholic apologists, especially here in America, are very eager to tell us right and left and at all occasions that far from being hostile to democracy, the Church, on the contrary, was its cradle—that even the democratic constitution of the United States derives in direct line from the teaching of Thomas Aquinas and of his sixteenth-century continuators and revisors.

You have noticed, I am sure, that in speaking of our democracy, I have used the term "modern democracy" and not democracy without qualifications. This distinction is of capital importance to avoid semantic mystifications and the consequent confusion of tongues. It is not here the place to discuss Aquinas's political theories. For our purpose, it will be enough to remark that in his system, the principle of the sovereignty of the people does not imply the direct responsibility of the government to the people, which is so fundamental to a modern democracy. Much less is there in Aquinas's system any room for the democratic freedoms of conscience, of religion, of thought and speech, the only mention of which would make Aquinas and his continuators turn in their graves.

As a matter of fact, when the Church was confronted with the new democratic or liberal constitutions adopted in the nineteenth century, even by Catholic countries, its first reaction was to reject with horror all political and religious innovations. In 1814 Pope Pius VII protested against the draft of a new French constitution (Apostolic Letter to the bishop of Tour, *Post tam diuturnam*, April 29, 1814) which he said had caused him an "extreme anguish" because "it not only permits freedom of conscience and of cult, but promises support and protection to the ministers of what are called the cults. By granting this freedom to all cults . . . the Church, the immaculate bride of Christ, is put on the same level with heretical sects and even with Jewish perfidy."

No less grieved was the pope by the grant of freedom of press, "a freedom which threatens faith and morals . . . and leads to inevitable ruin." In 1832 Pope Gregory XVI in his famous encyclical *Mirari vos* (August 15) stated,

> It is from the heresy of Indifferentism that the false and absurd theory worthy of madmen (delirium) derives which holds that freedom of conscience must be secured and guaranteed to everyone. This is a contagious error to which the path is opened by the absolute freedom of thought which is spreading everywhere for the ruin of the Church and of the state and which some, by an excess of impudence, dare to say that it is of advantage to the Church. . . . Connected with this is the freedom of the press, the most deadly and execrable freedom for which one cannot have enough horror. We shake with indignation considering by what monstrous doctrines or rather prodigies of errors we are crushed. . . . From them flows the curse that runs through the face of the earth and makes us shed tears.

Then Gregory goes on to condemn those "doctrines which shake the fidelity and submission due to kings and princes and which cause everywhere seditions. . . . The sacred precepts of Christian religion condemn the detestable pride of those disloyal men who, burning with evil passions, are bent to upset and destroy the rights of the authority of kings, bringing to the people slavery under the guise of liberty."

Of the many encyclicals of the long pontificate of thirty-two years of Gregory's successor Pius IX, condemning practically all the new trends of modern religious, philosophical, and political thought, I will quote only one passage from the Encyclical *Quanta Cura* of December 8, 1864, in which Pius stated:

> Contrary to the doctrine of the Scripture, of the Church and of the Holy Fathers, they [liberals and philosophers] are not afraid to affirm that the best government is that which does not impose upon the civil power the obligation to repress, by inflicting penalties, all violations of Catholic religion, except the case when repression is necessary for the preservation of public order. As a consequence of these false ideas on government, they do not hesitate to stand for . . . what our predecessor of happy memory, Gregory XVI, called a *delirium*, that is to say, the teaching that freedom of conscience and of cults is a right of everyone, that this freedom must be proclaimed and secured in every well ordered state and that the citizens have the right to enjoy full liberty to express frankly and in public their opinion, whichever they may be, through free speech, free press, and other means, without any interference or limitation imposed by either the ecclesiastical or the civil authorities. By holding these false ideas, they countenance a freedom of perdition, because if it should always be permitted to human opinions to engage in conflicts, there

> would always be people daring to resist truth and
> to put their confidence in the babblings of human
> wisdom, a very dangerous conceit which Chris-
> tian faith and wisdom must avoid at any cost, in
> conformity with the teaching of our Lord Jesus
> Christ himself.

Like his predecessor, Pius IX stood firm in advocating the union of the throne and the altar as the only way to save the monarchies and the Church from the onslaught of the liberal and democratic forces.

His successor, Leo XIII, in the encyclicals of the early period of his pontificate, followed the same line. In his first encyclical, *Quod Apostolici* (December 28, 1878), he rejected disdainfully the principle of the equality of men as far as their civic rights and duties were concerned. Dealing with the principle of authority and its abuses by rulers, Leo stated, "If it happens that a ruler exceeds willfully in the exercise of his power, Catholic doctrine does not permit any insurrection by the people against him, in order to avoid greater evils. And if the excesses of the ruler reach the point that no hope of salvation is left, Christian patience teaches us that in such a case a remedy should be sought only in insisting prayers to God."

In his second encyclical, *Diuturnum* (June 29, 1881), the Pope repudiated the modern notion of the sovereignty of the people "which sets the authority on flimsy foundations and causes seditions and revolutions." In the next encyclical, *Humanum genus* (April 20, 1884), Leo condemned once more the doctrine that men have equal rights, as well as the theory that "all powers reside in the free people and those who govern do so by a delegation or concession made by the people, in such a way that if the popular will changes, those who govern may be dismissed, even against their will."

Political theories seem to have been a favorite subject with Pope Leo, but his best known, and more often quoted among his encyclicals on government, is the *Immortale Dei* (November 1, 1885). By this time Leo XIII, having set his mind to the task of lifting up the political prestige of the Holy See from the depth to which it had fallen under his predecessor, realized more and more that the papacy could not any longer maintain its rigid intransigent position. Some concessions to the political and social ideas and institutions of modern time had to be made. Whereupon he threw overboard the dynastic legitimist entanglements of his predecessors and urged the French Catholics to forget their dispossessed kings and to rally around the republic. A few years later, in 1891, he discarded the old notions concerning the social question, recognized the rights of labor, the legitimacy of labor unions, and suggested a compromise between capital and labor.

In this encyclical of 1885, Pope Leo, starting from the old principle that a ruling power is necessary to any human society—and that this power comes from God who is the author of society—reaches the conclusion that this sovereign power to rule is not necessarily bound to any political form of government, provided that it is just and it is exercised to the benefit of the people. To fulfill these qualifications a state must first of all practice the public cult of the true God and profess the true religion. It is not difficult to find out which is the true religion. Prophecies, miracles, the propagation of faith, and the testimony of the martyrs are clear evidence that the only true religion is that of Jesus Christ which is represented by the Catholic Church. God has divided the government of humanity between two powers, the ecclesiastical power and the civil power, and only harmony and collaboration of the two may secure world peace and prosperity. Given this condition—that the state recognizes, respects, and enforces the rights and claims of the Church—the Church is willing and ready to recognize and respect the state no matter what its political form may be. Thus, to the modern state which proclaims its indifference to the various forms of religion and cults, provided they respect the laws and remain within the constitutional boundaries of the state, Pope Leo opposed the indifference of the Church to the various political forms which the state may assume, be they monarchical, republican, or democratic, provided they guarantee the Church the enjoyment of all its rights, liberties, and privileges. On this condition, even a democratic regime would be agreeable to the Church.

This concession as to the external forms of government did not mean that the pope had changed his mind as to the constituent and fundamental elements of modern democracy. As a matter of fact, a long section of the encyclicals is devoted to a new refutation of those principles, which are presented as having had their original source in the Protestant rebellion against the Church and had spread with the French Revolution to the destruction of Christian and natural law. The first of these poisonous principles is that of the equal rights of the people. In a society based on this principle, public authority is the will of the people, which is the only ruler. It chooses its representatives in such a way that it delegates to them not the power, but only the function of ruling in the name of the people. The other false principles deriving from the first one are freedom of conscience, of the press, of secular education, the separation of church and state, and so on—all things which characterize the secular or lay state. On these points the pope repeats and confirms the teaching of his predecessors and of his previous encyclicals.

But while the Church—the pope adds—will always resist any limitation of its rights and powers by the state, it does not reject any form of government, or even the right of the people to have a greater or a lesser part in the government. The Church may even admit that, according to times and circumstances and under certain laws, such a regime may be to the advantage of the people and hence induce the obligation to be loyal to it. A certain amount of liberty, but not the liberty which ignores the laws of God and of the Church, is admissible; nay, it has always received the support of the Church.

As a conclusion, Pope Leo urged the Catholics the world over to take part in the political life of their countries, to try to get hold of the government and then to use it for the defense of the Church. "It is evident that Catholics have just reasons to get into politics; but they must do this, not because they can approve of what is deplorable in the present political institutions of their country, but in order to use those institutions in such a way as to secure the public good, and with the purpose of injecting in all the veins of the State, as a new vital blood, the virtue and the influence of the Catholic religion."

This encyclical which gave the impression that the papacy was at last willing to meet modern political institutions halfway created a great stir, especially among the young Catholic clergy. They began to speak right and left of a Christian democracy blessed by the pope. In their enthusiasm, they interpreted his words so broadly as to imply that he approved at least the essential tenets of a modern democratic system of government. Pope Leo, pleased by the success of his message, but not wishing to be misunderstood too much, issued another encyclical, *Libertas prestantissimum* (June 20, 1888), in which he explained, first, that human liberty means a liberty altogether subordinated to the laws of God and the laws of the Church. Then, he attacked once more the theories and practices of political liberalism, and once more he dealt with the democratic freedoms and made clear his thought about them. Freedom of conscience understood as the right to follow any religion that one may choose, or even to have no religion at all, the pope rejected most emphatically. He rejected, likewise, freedom of religion in the sense that the state should bestow equal rights on all religions, but here the pope made the concession that the Church does not object to a measure of tolerance "for certain things which are contrary to truth and justice, if these things are rigorously circumscribed." Also, in the matter of the freedom of press and of speech, Pope Leo was willing to relax somewhat the rigid policy of the Church and to consider feasible the grant of a limited freedom, provided the state should not allow any propaganda of false religions or attacks against the true religion. In the last part of this encyclical, the pope stated, this time more specifically, that

Catholics were allowed to prefer a democratic state constitution, always on condition that the Catholic doctrine on the origin and the exercise of the political power be respected.

Encouraged by these last words of the encyclical which suggested a more decisive and final papal approval, and still more by *Rerum novarum,* the encyclical on the social question published three years later, in 1891, the growth of the Christian democratic movement as a new political and social force in Catholic countries gained in intensity. Pope Leo had also imposed the adoption of Aquinas's philosophy in Catholic schools, but at the same time he urged students and professors to become acquainted with modern scholarly methods of research and historical criticism. He even opened the secret Vatican archives to qualified scholars. A keen revival of cultural traditions and a new eagerness to appropriate the methods and results of modern scholarship made their way into many Catholic seminaries and theological schools. Very soon, however, the watchdogs of orthodoxy began to discover in these movements dangerous innovations and heretical leanings.

It was not difficult for these reactionaries to show that Leo's teaching, taken as whole and set against the background of the traditional doctrines and policies of the Church, did not substantiate the claim made by Christian democrats and modernists that they were following the pontifical instructions and directions. The nonagenarian pontiff hesitated for a long time before he said his final word on this conflict. At last on January 18, 1901, a year before his death, he published his long and ponderous *Graves de communi,* the last of his large collection of encyclicals. The essential part of it is a detailed analysis of the content and meaning of Christian democracy. The young Christian democrats and many others with them were no little surprised when they read the conclusion reached by the pope in this analysis. "It is an error to be condemned," said Leo, "to give a political meaning to the name of Christian democracy. Undoubtedly the name 'democracy' according to its etymology and to its usage by philosophers means a regime of the people, but in the present circumstances it must be shorn of all political connotations and must be used with no other meaning than that of a beneficent Christian action among the people." This Christian action can be carried on under any form of government. In fact, Christian democracy in this sense is not a novelty; it has been in the program of the Church from the very beginning.

With this final tragic retreat from the slightly advanced positions previously taken, the long pontificate of Leo XIII came to an end. His successor, Pius X, who came from the reactionary ranks, clamped down with extreme severity on Christian democracy, and with his famous encyclical *Pascendi Dominici gregis* (September 8, 1907) condemning Modernism, shut again and firmly the door against all innovations.

After the First World War, when democracy seemed triumphant in the new political setup of Europe, Pope Benedict XV permitted the organization of Catholic political parties, which were expected to assume the task of looking after the interests of the Church in the parliaments and governments of the various countries. The results of this experiment were not encouraging to the Church because those Catholic parties claiming democratic autonomy at times refused to be controlled by the ecclesiastical hierarchy. Very soon, however, European democracy collapsed and was superseded in several countries by dictatorships under various names, but all were alike in trampling under their feet all vestiges of liberty. Pope Pius XI, Benedict's successor, smothered the Catholic democratic parties and preferred to deal with the dictators. He made concordats and agreements with them, which he thought would more successfully protect the interests of religion and of the Church. The most important of those concordats was that made with the fascist regime in Italy in February 1929. During his controversy with Mussolini about the interpretation of the concordat, Pope Pius, in a letter to Cardinal Pietro Gasparri, dated May 30, 1929, took the opportunity to denounce once more the principles of freedom of conscience (which, he said, is tantamount to "a denial that a creature is subject to the Creator") and of freedom of discussion, that is freedom of speech and the press. Such absolute freedom is not admissible if it includes the freedom of discussion and the propaganda of ideas contrary to the religion of the state (the Catholic religion). "If by freedom of conscience," the pope remarked, "is meant the recognition that conscience is not subject to the powers of the state, and the recognition that in matters of conscience the Church, and only the Church, is competent by a divine mandate, then it implies also the recognition that in a Catholic state, freedom of conscience and of discussion must be understood and practiced only according to the doctrine and the laws of the Catholic Church."

In these concordats made by Pius XI with Catholic states, the Vatican did not demand the suppression by law of religious tolerance; not even the new dictators could afford to erase from the statutes the principle of freedom of religion. But the Catholic Church was recognized as the Church of the religion of the state, enjoying special privileges and exemptions, and, above all, the financial support of the state for the maintenance of the clergy, of the cult, and in some cases of the ecclesiastical schools. Other religions and cults were tolerated, but their activities, and especially their religious propaganda, were severely repressed by special laws or by the police; their religious periodicals were suppressed, and strict limitations were imposed on their public worship.

The Second World War swept away the concordats of Pius XI. But the concordat made with fascist Italy has not only been preserved but has gained more solid ground by having become an integral part of the new Italian republican constitution. Although freedom of religion was guaranteed most emphatically by this new constitution, in fact, this freedom (as well as the fundamental democratic principles of the equality of all citizens before the law and of no discrimination against any individual or class of people for religious reasons) is ruled out in the same constitution by the state's recognition of the sovereignty of the Church and by several articles of the concordat. Among those provisions of the concordat, there is one which excludes those who have incurred the excommunication of the Church from holding any public office in the state, so that if one such person should be elected by the people to a seat in parliament, this election would be null and void because unconstitutional. Thus, in the twentieth century, a partial restoration of the power of coercion of the state at the disposal of the Church and of political discrimination for religious reasons took place in a so-called democratic constitution.

Moreover, the articles of the fascist penal code, which restrict under penalties the practice of non-Catholic churches, have not been revoked. The fascist law stripped non-Catholics of their freedom and prescribed that no churches or chapels may be established by non-Catholics unless they obtained a special authorization by the head of the government, who is free to refuse it if in his judgment there is no need for such a church or chapel. Even the fascist law on the Jewish cult, which obliges liberal and modernist Jews to pay a tribute to the orthodox synagogues, was not abolished. This is the idea of freedom and the type of democracy that is tolerated by the Catholic Church wherever it can impose its will.

Pope Pius XII on several occasions, during and after the war, has spoken in defense of the rights of the individual, even of democracy, and even of religious freedom. Some phrases uttered by him on these subjects sound rather unusual in the mouth of a pope and are in striking contrast with the language of his predecessors. Does this mean that the Catholic Church has now discarded the thesis or that it has yielded altogether to the hypothesis in its policy toward religious freedom and democracy? The policies followed by the pope in Italy, Spain, and Portugal are a clear indication—facts are more eloquent than words—that he has not. As a matter of fact, his general statements about freedom were suggested by the peculiar condition of certain countries, such as Soviet Russia, where freedom is denied to the Catholic Church and obstacles are raised to its propaganda and organization. As such, the utterances of the pope reenter the Catholic tradition which has always demanded freedom for the Catholic Church in non-Catholic countries, while restricting the freedom of non-Catholic religious organizations in Catholic countries.

This distinction between a Catholic and a non-Catholic country, which is so important in the Catholic program, was frankly discussed some time ago, by Mr. Hilaire Belloc, a French-born Catholic writer who, in America, came to rank after the Fathers of the Church in connection with the problem with which American religious life will be confronted if and when the Catholics form the majority of the population and control the political institutions of this country. Belloc *(Atlantic Monthly,* 1930) approaches the subject from a new and subtle distinction between a country in which there is a Catholic majority and a country which is "organically Catholic and not mechanically so." So far as countries of the former type are concerned, Mr. Belloc said, "The idea that a Catholic majority, in the modern political sense of the word, would impose Catholicism over a minority standing against it, is wildly wrong. But an organically Catholic country is amply justified by all Catholic principles in fighting the beginning of disruption within its own body; it is justified in making Catholic ideas, education, manners and all the rest of it, the rules of a Catholic state; it is amply justified in struggling long and hard to prevent the break up of Catholic society and to save the unity of its civilization."

In other words, the principle and practice of religious tolerance is admissible in countries where there is a numerical Catholic majority but the country as a whole is not organically Catholic. However, an organically Catholic country has the right, nay the duty, to be intolerant and not permit the propaganda or even the existence of non-Catholic religions. The United States, said Mr. Belloc, is at present a non-Catholic country and freedom of religion fits well its condition and needs. It is probable that in a not very distant future the Catholics here may form the majority of the population, but still the country will not be organically Catholic and hence this majority will not have the right to force Catholicism over the minority of non-Catholics. Only with the passing of generations in the far away future, if ever, America may become organically Catholic. But why worry about this distant future event which might never occur? Let the American non-Catholics sleep peacefully and not be disturbed by the nightmare of the Inquisition and the burning of heretics.

Mr. Belloc's distinction between a country that has a Catholic majority and one that is organically Catholic is more imaginary than real. No community, whether of a religious, political, economic, or charitable character, is ever a simple aggregation of individuals set mechanically side by side as the grains in a bushel. A Catholic majority in any country is and will always be an organized majority. This is especially true of a Catholic majority because a close hierarchical organization is essential to a Catholic community. Otherwise it ceases to be Catholic.

Furthermore, Mr. Belloc's theory that an organically Catholic country, whatever this may mean, has the right to start religious persecutions is subversive of all the elementary principles of progress and civilization. There is no reason why the same right should be denied to any other country which is organically Protestant or organically pagan. Mr. Belloc seems to accept this corollary when he states that "any established society, good or evil, possesses rights," which in this case would mean the "right" to oppose any change, even for good. If this is true, then we cannot blame the Roman government for persecuting the Christians because Roman society was organically pagan, and we cannot blame the American English colonies for excluding the Catholics because these colonies were organically Protestant. And since to every right there is a correlated duty, we should add that the Christians did wrong in Christianizing the Roman Empire and that the Catholics should have abstained from introducing the Catholic faith in the English colonies.

But apart from these inconsistencies, Mr. Belloc's position, in spite of its charitable intentions and its final justification of intolerance, runs against the official Catholic teaching concerning non-Catholic countries. The rules of conduct and the program of action imposed by the Church to the clergy and laity living in such countries are given in detail in the textbooks on Church law and on moral theology in all Catholic ecclesiastical schools. Let us turn to the textbook on Public Ecclesiastical Law[1] of the Pontifical Gregorian University, where the young American seminarians who go to the American College in Rome get their training.

According to this textbook, all Catholics living in a state which grants to all religions equal freedom and rights before the law

> have the duty to render to the Church all the services which should be but are not rendered by the

state . . . and supply the Church with the means for a decent maintenance of the clergy, of the cult, and of religious and charitable institutions. Last, but not least, Catholics must make all possible efforts to bring about the rejection of this religious indifference of the state and the instauration, as soon as possible (*quamprimum*) of the wished for union and concord of state and Church which will greatly contribute to the good of the state itself. To do these things rightly, it is necessary that Catholics should act in agreement helping each other, and should organize themselves and be united. They shall form associations, hold public meetings and congresses, publish newspapers and magazines to assert and vindicate the rights of the Church and of religion. But all these activities must be carried on under the absolute control of the ecclesiastical authorities, obeying faithfully and with the whole heart their orders and never departing from them under any pretext.

The learned canonist Cavagnis, who later was made a cardinal, dealing with the same subject, expressed the opinion that if in a state, religious freedom or tolerance and equality of all religions is established by a statutory law under promise or oath to observe it, Catholics are bound to observe it faithfully as long as the non-Catholics have not disappeared. But the textbook condemns this opinion, because "whether tolerance of non-Catholic religions is promised under oath by a statutory law or not, it can never be admitted; hence what must be considered is only whether the abolition of tolerance is practically possible or not. The oath as such does not carry any obligation to permit a false religion."

According to this teaching, American Catholics under the orders of their hierarchy have the religious and moral duty to undermine, by all means, the American system of religious freedom and equality of all religions before the law, and to bring about a union of the Catholic Church and the state in this country. Are the American Catholics fulfilling this duty? We will turn to history for an answer to this question.

3

AMERICAN CATHOLICISM IN THE NINETEENTH CENTURY

The expansion of Catholicism in the United States, in a period relatively so short and on such a large territorial extension, has no parallel in the whole history of modern Christianity. In 1789, when the first American Catholic bishopric was established in Baltimore, there were in the regions then forming the United States about 15,000 Catholics, assisted by a dozen priests, former members of the suppressed Jesuit order, and by a few other missionaries. In 1949, according to the statistics of the Catholic Church, there were in the United States about 26 million Catholics, gathered in more than 100 dioceses, to which new ones were added almost every year, and ruled by a hierarchy of over 150 bishops and archbishops, 4 of them being members of the Roman College of Cardinals. After the Italian, the American Catholic episcopal body was known as the largest in the whole Catholic Church.

Almost to the end of the nineteenth century, when the Catholic Church in the United States was still ranked as a church of missions under the special jurisdiction of the Roman Congregation *de Propaganda Fide*, bishops, apostolic prefects, and vicars in America often needed financial subsidies from various missionary organizations of Europe and from Rome. Nowadays the situation is reversed. It is the American Church that now contributes on a large scale to the maintenance of the central government of the Church in Rome, and to the support of large missionary undertakings in South America and in the Far East. Above all, it is now the American Church that contributes the largest share of subsidies to the Holy See (Peter's Pence), while most other churches throughout the Catholic world, in the straitened circumstances following World War II, could afford to give but little or nothing.

For the first time in its long history the Catholic Church has made, in the United States on a large scale and for a considerable length of time, the great experiment of living under and adapting itself to a political regime of democratic freedom, of complete religious liberty, and of friendly separation of church and state. It is then very important to find out whether and how far the Catholic Church in the United States has been affected by the democratic climate, the democratic institutions, and the American way of life, and vice versa: whether and how far American institutions, American thought, and the religious, social, and political programs of American democracy have felt the influence of Catholicism, at least from the time in which the Catholic Church has become a compact, well disciplined, and numerically strong religious body, with a social, economic, and political program of action striving to gain control of American life.

The modern Catholic Church of America was a new creation of the nineteenth century. The Catholic missions of the colonial period, remarkable as they were for the heroic zeal of some of its missionaries and their geographical discoveries, left only a few traces here and there in the regions which later formed the United States. The foundation of a permanent Catholic Church and its growth were due primarily to Catholic immigrants and their clergy, especially the Irish, who during the nineteenth century, in ever increasing migratory currents, settled in the United States.

As in Christian Rome of the first centuries, likewise in America, Catholicism was at first, and remained for a long time, the religion of immigrant groups guided and ruled by an imported clergy. In Rome, however, Christianity imported from the eastern regions of the Empire and confronted with pagan religions and cults, began in its relatively early stage to gain ground among the Latin local population, making converts even in the high classes. Finally, having secured first the recognition and then the support of the government, it rapidly increased its ranks by mass conversions. In America, on the contrary, where Catholicism found itself confronted with Protestant Christianity, the dominant religion of the country, there was no considerable penetration of the Catholic faith either in the low or in the high classes of the Protestant population, and much less were there mass conversions. The rapid growth of the Catholic population was due not to new local conquests made by the Church, but to the incoming stream of Catholic immigrants from Ireland, southern Germany and the Rhine provinces, and later on from Italy and the Mediterranean countries, from Austria and Poland and other central European nations.

The most urgent and imperative task of the Catholic Church in America during the whole nineteenth century was not that of making converts from Protestantism, but rather that of not losing its own followers who came, wave after wave, from Europe and settled in this country from the Atlantic to the Pacific. But they were too many, and they came in too rapid succession, while the means and the available clergy were too few to care for all of them. There were severe losses which only in a small part were offset by conversions.

As ancient Christianity in the Roman Empire, so Catholicism in America was and remained for a long time an urban religion, a religion which flourished in the great industrial cities of the Atlantic shoreline and then in the cities which grew up throughout the continent to the Pacific. The rural regions remained, and are still, in a great majority, Protestant. The Irish immigrants and later on those from other countries settled by preference in the cities, where they could more easily find work in the growing American industries, and where the gregarious spirit peculiar to all immigrants could more easily be satisfied.

These large agglomerations of immigrants from all countries, all races, and all religions, cruelly exploited by their employers, gave rise to the slums of the American industrial cities where, among others, thousands of Catholic families lived in deplorable hygienic and moral conditions. In all those cities, and everywhere a nucleus of even a few hundred Catholic families were to be found, Catholic parishes and bishoprics were established in rapid succession. But the bishops did not encourage attempts which were made to direct the flow of Catholic immigration toward the rural regions; they were afraid that those immigrants, in the midst of a Protestant population and without the regular assistance of a resident priest, would run the risk of losing their faith.

Finally, like Christianity in ancient Rome, Catholicism in America met with the hostility of the local population. This hostility, however, never assumed in America the form of a bloody persecution. In colonial times the public Catholic cult was forbidden. Catholics were often expelled from certain regions. In others they were deprived of political rights, with the exception of a short period in the colony of Maryland. They were, also, usually tolerated by the Quakers of Pennsylvania. The proclamation of independence and the adoption of the principle of religious freedom abolished all these restrictions. But the hostility toward Catholics as subjects of a foreign and enemy power, the papacy, which was believed to have sinister designs over America, continued, and went even through periods of recrudescence, with riots and burning of some convents and churches. In reality, these outbursts of violence were due not only to the old fanatic British tradition of "No popery!" but also to a current of xenophobia which usually appears in countries where the population has grown through successive layers of immigrants and where the older layers, resenting the invasion of the newcomers, react violently against them. But gradually all open hostility at least, if not anti-Catholic prejudices and suspicions, died out.

It must be said also that Catholicism, which for a long time was represented primarily by poor immigrants who had no influence upon the intellectual and political life of the country, did not inspire any fear among a large section of the dominant class. What the wealthy class was afraid of was, rather, the danger arising from large masses of poor people without any religious and moral rein. Thus it often happened that wealthy Protestants contributed to the erection of Catholic churches and chapels, holding the utilitarian view that religion, any religion, helps to keep the low classes in their place.

The American statesmen who framed the American Constitution and the elected representatives of the nation who adopted it, though they were Protestants with only very few exceptions, refrained from making the Protestant faith the state religion of the nation, as it had been in the colonies. They acknowledged and sanctioned the right of individuals and groups to adopt any religion, or no religion at all, as they wished, as well as the right to enjoy all the privileges granted by law to all citizens irrespective of religious affiliation. To prevent conflicts caused by the mutual penetration of religion and politics, and to solve the problem of relations of church and state in a nation of divided religious allegiance, they very wisely sanctioned the principle that Congress should have no authority to make laws concerning the establishment of any religion. By this they intended to raise a wall marking the separation of the spheres of action of religion on the one side and of the state on the other.

These principles were gradually adopted by the various states of the federation in their constitutions. The disestablishment of the church was a heavy blow for those Protestant churches which had enjoyed, up to that time, a position of privilege in, and financial support by, the state. On the contrary, it was a blessing for such religions as Catholicism which, up to that time, had not even gained a legal recognition of their right to exist. To the Protestant church, the separation of church and state meant a demotion from their official status to the condition of private organizations; to the Catholic Church, it was a promotion from an organization discriminated against to the status of perfect legal equality with all other religious organizations. All churches were left to depend upon their own resources, free to compete against each other on equal terms, as far as the law of the land was concerned.

As far as the churches were concerned, one of the first results of the proclamation of independence in America was the breaking of the ties which up to that time had bound several religious denominations with mother churches or religious bodies of Europe, and especially of England. Thus the Anglican Church became the autonomous Episcopal Church of America with its own hierarchy; other denominations organized their synods or other organs of government with complete freedom to fix their creeds, their statutes, and their rules of discipline according to their needs. But it was not so with the Catholic Church, since in the Catholic system there is no room for autonomy.

In the colonial period, the Catholic mission entrusted to the Jesuits in Maryland, and in other British colonies to which they had access, was under the jurisdiction of the Apostolic Vicar in London. The same year that the American Revolution began, Pope Clement XIV suppressed the order of the Jesuits, and so the missionaries found themselves at once cut off from all connections with the London Vicar and without any superior of the order. They were left to themselves. When peace was reestablished, the connection of the mission with London was not restored, but the mission was put under the direct dependence of the Roman Congregation for the Propagation of the Faith, which in 1784 appointed one of the ex-Jesuits, John Carroll, head of the mission, with the title of Apostolic Prefect. John Carroll, who came from a wealthy family of Maryland, was held in great esteem by George Washington and other leaders of the revolution, and during the war rendered valuable service to the cause of independence. And yet, he was so afraid that his appointment made in Rome might cause an unfavorable reaction in the authorities and in American public opinion, that he notified only the clergy and not the laity of his promotion. The reorganization of the mission led soon to the establishment of an American bishopric. The fact that the election of the bishop had to come from Rome, and the possibility that Rome might send a foreigner to lead the American Church, caused a great deal of anxiety to Carroll and his small clergy. In February 1785 Carroll wrote to the Cardinal of Propaganda as follows:

> In most places Catholics are not admitted to any office in the State unless they renounce all foreign jurisdiction, civil or ecclesiastical. . . . The Catholic body here thinks that some favor should be granted to them by the Holy Father, necessary for their permanent enjoyment of the civil rights which they now enjoy. . . . Your Eminence must see how objectionable all foreign jurisdiction is to them [the authorities and people]. . . . We hope

that some plan may be adopted by which here-
after an ecclesiastical superior may be appointed
for this country, in such a way as to retain
absolutely the spiritual jurisdiction of the Holy
See, and at the same time remove all ground of
objecting to us, as though we held anything hostile to the national independence.

The plan which Carroll had in mind and which he later on submitted to Rome was that the American clergy be granted the privilege to choose the bishop and the city of his residence. Rome hesitated but finally granted this privilege only for this case. Baltimore was chosen as the seat of the first American bishopric and John Carroll himself as the first bishop. The same year, 1789, the Philadelphia Convention promulgated the new Constitution of the United States.

A few years later, the need was felt of dismembering the immense diocese of Baltimore and establishing new bishoprics in New York, Philadelphia, and Boston. Carroll and his priests sent to Rome the names of their candidates, but Rome accepted their choice only in part; the same thing happened again and again in the erection of new bishoprics.

This question of the election of bishops remained undecided for a long time. The American clergy insisted on advocating the privilege of episcopal nominations in order to avoid unfavorable reactions of American public opinion. The bishops and the clergy of Ireland, since the majority of American Catholics were Irish, wished to secure for themselves the monopoly of American bishoprics, and they very often succeeded in Rome in imposing their candidates. Last but not least,

Rome, while recognizing the difficult position of the American bishops, did not wish that the privilege granted in a special case should become a permanent right of the American Church.

This attempt made by the American clergy, under the influence of American public opinion and democratic institutions, to restore in their church the ancient ecclesiastical discipline in which the bishops were elected primarily by the clergy, ended in a failure. However, it left a trace in the practice (adopted later on) by which at the death of a bishop the local clergy and the bishops of the province were allowed to submit a list of three names, from whom Rome could, if it wished, select the new bishop. Even this slight participation of the clergy in episcopal nomination was abolished in 1908 when Pius X decreed that the Church in America was no longer a missionary church and submitted it to the general regulations of Canon Law.

Much more important and more significant was the long and sharp conflict of Catholic laymen with their bishops. This conflict is known by the name of trusteeism. When the Catholics began to build churches and chapels with the contributions of the faithful, they followed the usual legal procedure, as Protestants do, to form a corporation which owns the church and administers it through trustees elected by the congregation. These Catholic laymen, who as trustees administered the temporal affairs of their churches, began very soon to claim the right, as in the Protestant churches, to choose their own pastors and to dismiss them whenever they wished to do so. But according to Canon Law, this is an exclusive right of the bishop, who alone can give the canonical investiture and the powers of spiritual administration to a parish priest. These conflicts, which kept the Catholic Church in a turmoil, lasted many years. The trustees locked the doors of the church to keep out both the priests sent by the bishops and the bishops themselves. The bishops reacted by interdicting the churches and excommunicating the rebels. The resistance of the trustees went on, and they even asked to have a voice in the election of bishops.

Behind this revolutionary attempt to introduce in Catholic discipline something like a democratic system of elections, and thus to secure for the laymen a certain power in the administration of the Church, there was also another element which we may call nationalistic. The scarcity of priests had been, from the beginning, the greatest handicap of the American church; but during the French Revolution not a few French clergy, some of them men of large culture and of great zeal, came to America and became the right hand of Bishop Carroll, who had several of them promoted to newly created bishoprics. Gradually Irish priests also began to come in increasing ranks, as well as some German priests who accompanied groups of German Catholics who settled first in Pennsylvania and then in other American regions. It does not require a great stretch of imagination to understand that the Irish, who formed the greatest majority of the Catholic population, very often could not stomach being under the spiritual guidance of French priests or French bishops. Furthermore, in many cases, behind the rebel trustees there were some restless, ambitious Irish priests willing to accept their nomination as rectors of parishes made by the trustees and openly to challenge the authority of the bishop. Likewise, the Germans wanted only German priests and bishops. The bishops, harassed by these rebellions and fearing that they might have turned into permanent schism, tried to reestablish peace by some compromise, but having failed, they were forced more and more to assume an intransigent attitude.

The first Provincial Council of Baltimore (1829) passed a decree forbidding the erection and consecration of any church unless, *when possible*, it had been first deeded to the bishop of the place. This law, which provided for the future and only when possible, had little or no effect. Almost all the subsequent provincial and then the Plenary Councils of Baltimore issued regulations on this point. There were two questions to be solved: One was how to bring all ecclesiastical properties under the direct control of the bishops, eliminating the troublesome interference of lay trustees; the other concerned the safest method of holding such property by the bishops according to the laws and prescription of the various American states.

As to the first point, it was necessary not only to prevent the formation of new corporations with lay trustees, which could be done by a strict enforcement of the decree of 1829, but also to bring under the absolute control of the bishops, or eliminate altogether, the existing lay corporations. These corporations, however, had a legal existence, and when in several cases recourse was made to the civil courts of the state, the rights of ownership of the corporation and their trustees had been sustained by the law. This vexed question was thoroughly threshed out at the second Plenary Council of Baltimore in 1866 reaching the conclusion that "in order to obtain protection from the improper interference of lay tribunals, which in practice scarcely acknowledge the ecclesiastical laws, nothing now remains to the bishops for carrying out ecclesiastical decrees but to claim for themselves the fullest administration of property before the civil law." The bishops' point of view was that, since in the United States all citizens are free to live according to the precepts of their religion, no obstacle should be raised by the law to the exact observance by the Catholics of the decrees of councils and popes for the legitimate acquisition and preservation of ecclesiastical property. "Complete liberty can be said to exist only when the laws and ordinances of the church are recognized by the civil tribunals and thus receive civil effects." Whereupon the bishops stated their firm decision to see to it "that the right of the Church be vindicated in the eyes of all and publicly before the state." Their efforts were crowned by success because in subsequent cases submitted to the lay courts, the bishops' contention was upheld by the judges on the basis that a religious corporation is bound to observe the statutes of the religious body to which it belongs; and that by the statutes of the Catholic Church (Canon Law), the bishops had the right to control ecclesiastical properties.

As to the second point, the third Plenary Council of Baltimore prescribed that the safest methods of ownership according to civil law are (1) The bishop himself be constituted a corporation sole for possessing and administering the property of the whole diocese; (2) the bishop hold the property in trust in the name of the diocese; (3) the bishop hold and administer the property in his name (in fee simple) by an absolute and legal title. In such cases, however, the bishop had to observe special ecclesiastical regulations to make sure that the property would go at his death to his legitimate successor. This method has now been practically discarded. With some slight modifications introduced later on, the first two are still the methods by which the bishops own, administer, or control directly the administration and use of all the ecclesiastical properties in the United States.

This episode throws a great deal of light on the general trend of the institutional life of the Catholic Church in its development in the United States. The early endeavor of Carroll and his early successors to secure for the high clergy the nomination of bishops and the attempt of the trustees to have a part in the nomination of pastors, reviving thus in America the system of election to ecclesiastical offices of the ancient Church, failed altogether. In matters of ecclesiastical property, on the contrary, the American Church went back to, and revived even more rigidly, the system of the ancient Church when the creation and separate endowment of ecclesiastical benefices had not yet begun and all ecclesiastical possessions and incomes were administered directly by the bishops. In the ancient Church also, the ownership of ecclesiastical properties, in the eyes of Roman law, was vested in local corporations until the time when the Church as such was recognized as having a moral and juridical personality (as found already in the legislation of Justinian). In the United States, the situation of the Catholic Church in the matter of property is, broadly speaking, that of the pre-Justinian times with the right of ownership vested in local corporations which, however, are formed or directly controlled by the bishops and not by the congregations of the faithful.

As a matter of fact, in the American Catholic Church neither the institution of patronage, already rejected by the Council of 1829, nor that of ecclesiastical benefices canonically erected and having patrimonial possessions and autonomous administration, were ever introduced. Being a missionary church, and as such exempted from the general institutional regulations of Canon Law, the American Church did not establish cathedral chapters or colleges of canons and not even parishes, according to the rules of the Council of Trent (1545–1563), having a legal existence and personality of their own.

In the American Church all the offices and ecclesiastical positions are filled by a direct episcopal appointment, and the bishop can dismiss, remove, or transfer all such officers from one place to another. The Third Plenary Council of Baltimore (1884) created a class of *irremovable rectorships* (10 percent of all parishes) the holders of which form a body of consultors to help the bishop in his administration. But their parishes, like all others, are not canonically erected, and are called in Canon Law *quasi-parishes.* Their rectors are called *quasi-parochi,* having all the duties and responsibilities of the office, but not all the privileges and guarantees of the canonically instituted parochial benefices.

As a result of this system of diocesan government, the American bishop has absolute powers over his clergy because it is he who controls the whole ecclesiastical property and its administration, while in the exercise of his authority he is not restricted by institutional beneficiary rights and autonomous traditions. To compensate the American clergy for the lack of canonships and other distinctions which entitle such dignitaries of the Church to wear special robes, gold crosses, and miters, such as decorate the clergy of old Europe, the American bishops in recent times have solicited and obtained a rainfall of special honorary titles bestowed by the Vatican such as "Secret Chamberlain of His Holiness," or, "Domestic Prelate of the Pope," all of which entitle the bearer to wear silk violet robes and to be called a monsignor. These distinctions, which seem to have a peculiar fascination in democratic America, serve the double purpose of bestowing recognition based on merit and of binding the American clergy more closely to Rome.

The second half of the nineteenth century marked the transition of the American Catholic Church from its infancy to a vigorous youth, of which its spectacular expansion is witness. The outstanding events which affected the life of the Church in the United States during that period were the abolitionist controversy followed by the Civil War, the intensification of Catholic immigration, the rise of the labor movement, the establishment of the Apostolic Delegation in Washington, and the condemnation by Pope Leo XIII of the so-called Catholic Americanism.

According to the traditional teaching of the Church from ancient times, slavery is neither against the law of nature, nor against the positive law of God revealed in the Old and New Testaments. As long as the whole economic life of peoples and nations was dependent upon slave labor, and slavery appeared to be a normal and inevitable institution, it would have been preposterous to expect that Christianity or any other religion should have challenged its legitimacy and its existence. But beside teaching the spiritual equality of people called all alike to achieve salvation, the Church drew up a code of morals which sanctioned, on the one hand, the moral duty of the slave to be obedient and faithful to his master, and on the other hand the strict obligation of the master to treat his slave with human and spiritual kindness. Moreover, the Church encouraged the manumission of slaves as a work of mercy. But by a strange twist of history, such as occurs when a religious institution becomes also a political and economic power, the Church, when it became itself a wealthy landowner and possessor of slaves, made the emancipation of these slaves very difficult by the strict laws in general forbidding the alienation of ecclesiastical properties.

As you know well, slavery in America had its origin in the criminal traffic of the African Negroes enslaved by force or deceit. But whatever its origin, it had become an established institution deemed necessary to the economic life of a large section of the country, and it was not abolished in spite of the fundamental principle of the natural and legal equality adopted by the Declaration of Independence.

Pope Gregory XVI in his encyclical *In Supremo Apostolatu* of 1839 stated once more the teaching of the church concerning slavery and condemned the slave traffic. The Catholic hierarchy in America shared the pope's view. Though some of them, such as Bishop England of Charleston, were ready to admit that American slavery was the greatest social and moral evil of the country, all of them were convinced that it was impossible and undesirable to abolish it in the existing circumstances. All of them were in agreement that freedom could be granted to slaves only after a long period of preparation and education and by a gradual process through successive steps.

During the long controversy which began to rend apart the United States, the Catholic clergy and the Irish Catholic masses in general joined the ranks of antiabolitionism and carried on in their press a campaign of sharp denunciation and at times of vituperation against the abolitionist movement. The *Boston Pilot* especially distinguished itself in this campaign by putting together in a bunch, as atheists and morally despicable people, the Bostonian group of high-minded thinkers and religious leaders who had taken a stand for abolition and the rabble of fanatics who were not lacking on both sides of the fence. One of the reasons given by Catholic historians to explain this strong antiabolitionist standing of American Catholicism had to do with economic and social factors of that time. The greatest majority of the Catholics belonged then to the hardworking classes struggling through periods of unemployment or low wages. It is understandable that they should fear that the sudden emancipation of millions of slaves would throw at once on the market such a superabundance of labor as to make inevitable large-scale unemployment and the sinking of wages down to a lower level since the Negroes would be satisfied to receive much less than white workers. A mass migration of free Negroes to the Northern states, where they could more easily find work, was also looked upon as an inevitable outcome of their emancipation.

When the Civil War started, the bishops of the Southern states remained faithful to the Confederation, while those of the Northern states maintained their allegiance to the Union. This division along political lines did, however, not imply any schism or separation of the two sections of the

Catholic Church, as happened with most Protestant denominations. Bishop Patrick Lynch of Charleston accepted the mission to go to Rome and to obtain from the pope, as temporal sovereign, the recognition of the secessionist Republic. On the other side, Archbishop John Hughes of New York, the energetic fighting Irishman as he was called, who had warned the government in Washington that Irish Catholics would refuse to fight for the emancipation of the slaves and would fight only for the maintenance of the union, accepted likewise a semi-official mission to Rome to neutralize the action of his colleague of Charleston. In fact Archbishop Hughes, reaching Rome, found out that his mission was superfluous because Bishop Lynch had completely failed to get even a hearing from the pope.

In spite of Hughes's pessimistic forecast, the Irish Catholics of the Northern states answered the call of the government and paid their share of blood and sacrifices for the cause of the union, even when it was no longer possible to separate it from the cause of emancipation. When the abolition of slavery became an accomplished fact by President Abraham Lincoln's proclamation, Bishop John Baptist Purcell of Cincinnati was the first to break the ice and to express his deep satisfaction that the stain of slavery had been wiped away once and for all from free, democratic America.

Of greater importance was the final policy adopted by the American Catholic Church toward the social question. It is not necessary to be reminded that the popes speaking for the Catholic Church condemned socialism and communism as soon as these theories made their appearance in Europe. From Pope Pius VI to the present Pope, Pius XII, the anathema of the Church had unalterably followed every forward step made by these movements, especially from the time in which they passed from the merely theoretical stage to the stage of action, by the formation of socialist and communist political parties, and later on by assuming control of the government in several countries. The condemnation of the Church was directed not only against the essentially materialistic conception of life and of history which was at the basis of socialist and communist theories, but also against their fundamental economic and social theory concerning private property. According to the Church, the right to private property is based on natural and divine law, and any attempt to destroy this right is a sacrilegious violation of all religious and moral principles.

The traditional teaching of the Church concerning the economic and social inequality of human beings was, briefly, that wealth for some and poverty for others is a normal and permanent condition of society, being part of the divine plan of government of humanity. A partial solution of this problem is to be found in the Christian precepts which, on the one hand, urge upon the rich the moral obligation to be generous and to give to the poor out of their superfluous means and, on the other hand, urge upon the poor to accept with resignation the divine will that they should suffer with patience the liabilities of poverty, and find consolation in the thought that poverty may be a blessing inasmuch as it makes it easier for them to gain eternal salvation. The sublime example given by Jesus, who chose for himself the lot of the poor, was always quoted as a final evidence of the spiritual advantages of poverty over wealth and the material things of life. Several encyclicals issued by Pius IX during his long pontificate urge upon the faithful again and again the observance of these divine laws as the only way to establish peace and harmony among the social classes.

Pope Leo XIII in his first encyclical, *Quod Apostolici* (December 28, 1878), repudiated again "socialists, communists and nihilists," these "sects having barbaric names," and all having the same purpose of destroying religion and civil society, and he made, once more, a passionate appeal for the observance of the divine laws: "The Church makes it a strict duty for the rich to give their superfluous to the poor, and she frightens them with the thought of the divine judgment which shall condemn them to eternal fire if they do not provide for the needs of the poor. She also uplifts and offers consolation to the spirit of the poor by proposing to them the example of Jesus Christ who, being rich, both made himself poor for us, and declared that blessed are the poor, who were given the hope of attaining eternal happiness."

It is not difficult to realize how inadequate this remedy appeared to be at a time when socialism in almost a century of slow but constant development had gained much ground, and thirty years had gone by since the publication of Marx's *Communist Manifesto.* The churches in America, both Protestant and Catholic, had paid little or no attention to the fact that just then a horde of financial adventurers and unscrupulous businessmen and bankers were rapidly accumulating fabulous fortunes by cleverly disguised thefts and by inhumanly exploiting the working classes. The churches not only ignored this problem, but when the agitations of the workers for higher wages and less exhausting and more decent working conditions began, churchmen who often owed to the rich the support of their parishes aligned themselves with the forces of exploitation and reaction. Mr. Aaron Abell says in his valuable book *The Urban Impact on American Protestantism*, "The workingmen lost confidence in a church that was in active or passive alliance with their oppressors." Then he quotes a passage from a pamphlet written in 1884 by John Swinton, a New York socialist, who said, "In the struggles of workers for better conditions during the panic years of the seventies, no clergyman was ever to be found. Each preferred to snuff the odors of fortune and cross their clerical limbs under the banquets of Nabobism, rather than to do as He whom they pretend to serve did."

Not much different was the attitude of the Catholic clergy, frightened by the menace of a social revolution. As Cardinal George William Mundelein said in an address in 1938, referring to this early period of great social unrest, "The trouble with us (Catholics) in the past has been that we were too often allied or drawn into an alliance with the wrong side. Selfish employers of labor have flattered the Church by calling it a great conservative force, and then called upon it to act as a police force, while they paid but a pittance of wage to those who worked for them."

Of course there were exceptions: In several European countries as well as in America, there were both Protestant and Catholic clergy who, living in close contact with and ministering to the poor classes, had become fully aware of the need of a united effort on the part of the workers. But they found no support; nay, they were usually disavowed by their churches. The first large and effective organization of workers in the United States was the Knights of Labor in the early 1880s. It had no religious or political character; Protestant and Catholic workers joined it, and its first president was a Catholic Irishman. Many Catholic bishops immediately raised their voices against it. They argued that the association of the Knights of Labor belonged to the class of secret societies forbidden by the Church, like Free Masonry and other organizations; that the association of Catholics with Protestants was also forbidden by the Church; and, last but not least, that in the program of the Knights of Labor was an element of socialism.

Only a small group of bishops led by James Gibbons of Baltimore and John Ireland of St. Paul, Minnesota, thought otherwise and approved of Catholic membership in that association. The matter was submitted to Rome by the reactionary bishops and by the bishops of Canada, who had unanimously condemned the Knights of Labor. Rome, after due consideration of the case, agreed with them. By order of Pope Leo, the Congregation of the Holy Office got ready the decree forbidding Catholics to join the association.

Warned in time by some Roman friend, Gibbons and Ireland rushed to Rome where they were joined by Cardinal Henry Edward Manning from London, and the three together respectfully submitted their opinion to the pope and pleaded the cause of labor. According to the official Italian biography of Leo XIII, Gibbons frankly warned the pope that the condemnation of the Knights of Labor would be disastrous to the Church because Catholic workers would not obey the order to withdraw from the association and would rather withdraw from the Church. The future of the

Church, said Gibbons, depends upon gaining to our side the masses of working people; if we shut the door in their face, they will desert us, and we will be left alone.

According to the same biographer, the pope was very much impressed by the words of the three prelates and suspended the publication of the decree. Having become aware of the opportunity offered to the Church to gain the working classes, Pope Leo began to study the problem. A few years later, in 1891, he published his famous encyclical *Rerum novarum*. Qualifying the attitude which he had taken at the beginning of his pontificate in the encyclical quoted above, Pope Leo recognized the right of the workers to resist exploitation, to form labor unions, and even to have recourse to strike when all other means to get just wages had failed. Of course, in the light of socialist and progressive programs of that period, Leo's encyclical was by no means original either in its criticism of the evils of the capitalist system or in the remedy which it suggested to obtain justice for the workers. But for the Catholic Church, it marked a great, bold step forward, breaking long-standing policies and putting in motion new Catholic forces on the side of labor. It was some time before the old clergy could adapt itself to this new way of looking at the social question.

Upon his return to the United States, Gibbons had no little difficulty in persuading the other bishops that the cause of labor was right. According to his biographers, looking back at those events, sometime later, the cardinal said, "Ah, what a struggle it was on both sides of the water! I had so many difficulties that I wonder I got through them. Bishops are hard to persuade! They have fixed and positive opinions, and I can scarcely imagine a class of men less easy to deal with on a subject of that kind."

For their attitude in this case, and in general for their open-mindedness on several other questions, Cardinal Gibbons and Archbishop Ireland gained a reputation for liberalism and progressivism. In reality, their attitude on this question was not dictated by liberal ideas as such. No Catholic churchman, and much less a high prelate, can afford to entertain views and theories which, like those of liberalism, run against the doctrinal or institutional traditions of their Church. What Gibbons and Ireland had primarily in mind was to prevent a blunder which would have been fatal to the American Church. In old Europe, where the Church possessed large endowments, or was supported by the state and leaned heavily on the aristocratic classes and the wealthy bourgeoisie, and where socialism and communism had openly assumed an antireligious character, the opposition of the Catholic hierarchy to the labor movement could be easily explained. But in America, where the Catholic Church was depending for its existence primarily on the working masses of Catholic immigrants and descendants of immigrants, of which only a few up to that time had climbed higher in the economic and social ladder, the repudiation by the Church of the labor movement could but end in a catastrophe. The masses of Catholic workers would have found themselves in a tragic dilemma: either quit the Church, or break the union front, earning the hatred of their non-Catholic brothers and being despised. Even the formation of exclusively Catholic labor unions, advocated by some members of the hierarchy, would have made the situation

worse by directly injecting the religious question in a conflict which was inevitably bound to have wide political and
social repercussions in all sections of American life.

Wiser and more far-seeing than their colleagues, Gibbons and Ireland were aware that a step back on the labor
question would have caused the Church, which they loved
and cherished, to lose all the gains made up to that time,
while a step forward would open the Church to new horizons and great new possibilities. Their liberalism, if we may
call it so, was strictly ecclesiastical, in the sense that they
were not afraid of new ideas and experiments when they
thought that they would further the interests of the American Church.

The last two decades of the nineteenth century are
described by American historians as a period of great
progress not only in the gigantic economic growth of the
country, but also in its cultural and social development. It
was at that time that our old colleges began to develop into
great universities and centers of learning. Moreover, new
colleges and a whole system of public schools, public
libraries and museums, and charitable and humanitarian
institutions came into existence in all sections of the
country. It was then that the working masses began to organize their unions more efficiently and to react in the name
of social justice against the exploitation of labor by the over-
powering industrial lords. It was then that the endless waves
of immigrants from all countries increased from year to
year, reaching its peak at the beginning of the new century
and raising new and formidable problems in the political,
social, and religious life of America.

The Catholic Church strongly felt the impact of these new active forces, especially of the great influx of Catholic immigrants from central and southern Europe who spoke no English and had no idea of American institutions and ways of life. It was necessary to establish new Catholic parishes and schools for them, and to import foreign priests, friars, and nuns. Every large American diocese became a collection of German, Italian, Polish, French-Canadian, Slavic, and Eastern Uniat churches, which in some places had larger congregations than the Irish-American parishes. To keep in line all these churches, often engaged in racial conflicts one against the other, and to curb the nationalistic tendency to perpetuate divisions by bringing up the children of immigrants in schools of foreign languages and traditions, was not an easy task. The problem of the absorption and Americanization of immigrants, which was then stirring American public opinion, was most disturbing to a church which was duty bound to provide spiritual assistance to the immigrants by allowing them to have churches of their own, isolating them from the rest of the American community, and unwillingly fostering their tendency to stick to their language, their traditions, and their foreign mentality.

Cardinal Gibbons, born in Baltimore, and Archbishop Ireland who, though born on the other side of the ocean, came to this country as a little boy, were the two most outstanding figures of American Catholicism of that period. Both of them were sincerely devoted to American democratic institutions. They believed that a regime of liberty was most favorable to the progress of Catholicism, unfettered by any political protection, and asking for no favors for which the Church inevitably had to pay a price. They felt that the Church in America, while remaining faithful to the doctrinal, moral, and institutional traditions and laws of Roman Catholicism, would gain much by the adoption of more modern American methods of approach to the spiritual and social problems of the American people.

Both Gibbons and Ireland were set against any attempt to perpetuate racial sectionalism in the American Church. Though they greatly appreciated the labors of bishops, priests, and members of religious orders, who had come from the other side of the ocean and had saved for the Church large masses of people and had helped so much in building up American Catholicism, the two American prelates were convinced that, as Gibbons said, "If the Church is to take deep roots in the country and to flourish, it must be sustained by men of the soil, educated at home, breathing the spirit of the country, growing with its growth, and in harmony with its civil and political institutions." A native clergy devoted to American democracy was their ideal.

Another striking personality in the Catholic clergy of that time was Fr. Isaac Hecker, of German descent, a convert and then founder of the religious society of the Paulist Fathers and of the Apostleship of the Catholic Press. Taught by his own spiritual and moral experience, Father Hecker conceived of Catholic life in the light of what could be called American activism. Especially in his technique for gaining converts, he was willing to adopt a certain doctrinal and spiritual latitude in the interpretation and application of normative Catholic traditions.

This ferment of new ideas in some advanced Catholic circles was in part connected with the European movement which had been encouraged by Leo XIII, and vice versa; it had no little influence on that very movement, especially through a series of lectures given by Ireland in France and through his writings, which were largely read in translations in France and Italy. To many European Catholics, the youthful American Church seemed to have assumed the task of blazing the way toward a broader vision of Catholicism as a modern progressive force, no longer encumbered by the medievalism of doctrinaires or by the legalistic sophistry of curialists.

In 1889, on the occasion of the centennial of the establishment of the Catholic hierarchy in the United States, the first congress of Catholic laymen was organized in Baltimore on the pattern of the European congresses then held periodically in various countries. Many precautions were taken to prevent any possible discordant note marring this first experiment of calling together the Catholic laity to express their faith and their readiness to work for the Church. The pope sent from Rome the Italian archbishop Francesco Satolli as his representative. The delegates to the Congress were not elected by the Catholic communities but were chosen very carefully by each bishop in his diocese. The papers to be read by them at the congress were first submitted to the censorship of a committee of bishops appointed by Gibbons, of which Ireland was the chairman. They dealt with a variety of topics such as education, Catholic press, Catholic societies, Catholic literature, art, and music. There was a paper by Charles Bonaparte in vindication of the temporal power of the popes. It seems that the idea of starting a Catholic political party in the United

States was ventilated by some laymen, but it was immediately quashed by Gibbons and his bishops. From the time of trusteeism, American Catholic laymen had been so subdued, and so resigned to play only a passive part in their church, that the bishops were now much surprised to find out that they could speak so well and so intelligently of matters usually reserved to the clergy. Archbishop Ireland, in the closing address to the congress, said frankly, "I am overjoyed to listen to such magnificent discourses and such grand papers, and to have realized that there is among our Catholics in America so much talent, so much strong faith. As one of your bishops, I am ashamed of myself that I was not conscious before this of the power existing in the midst of the laity, and that I have not done anything to bring it out. But one thing I will do with God's help. In the future I shall do all I can to bring out this power."

The second Catholic congress in the United States was held in 1893 in connection with the Columbus Exposition and World Fair's in Chicago. This time it was decided that only three main topics should be treated in the many papers to be read during the sessions: the social question as outlined by Leo XIII in the *Rerum novarum*, Catholic education, and the Independence of the Holy See, that is, the question of the temporal power of the popes. It was decided also not to allow discussion of the papers, as had been customary in such congresses. The Roman Question seems to have been an obligatory subject, though the only thing that American bishops and laymen could do was to pass platonic resolutions advocating the restoration of the temporal power and the breakdown of Italian political unity. It was part of Leo XIII's program to keep on stirring Catholic opinion the world over against Italy. The American Catholic Church had always denounced as criminal the Italian aspirations to independence and political unity, while the rest of the American people had followed the events of the Italian Risorgimento with a great deal of sympathy. Even Gibbons and Ireland, who professed devotion to liberty and democracy, were, if possible, more intransigent than the pope himself on this question of the temporal power of the Holy See.

The Vatican was highly pleased by this demonstration of loyalty, but it was not pleased at all by the statement made in some speeches that the Catholic Church in the United States should be American in character and should have a color and a personality of its own. Still more displeased was the pope by the fact that Gibbons and Ireland attended the Congress of Religions which was also held in Chicago in connection with the World's Fair, and which addressed the audience from the same platform with the representatives of all other religions. Shortly afterward Rome prescribed that the Catholic clergy were not permitted to attend such promiscuous religious congresses.

The central government of the Church had followed the establishment and the growth of the Catholic Church in the United States with a great deal of interest and with much satisfaction for its rapid progress, but not without misgivings. Rome feared that the boisterous spirit of independence, so peculiar to the new American nation, might infect the Catholic body. In 1852, bestowing the papal approval on the acts of the First Plenary Council of Baltimore, Rome warned the American bishops not to permit certain peculiar customs, which were followed by some American Catholic groups, to become general and be adopted uniformly by the whole American Church, for thus "the appearance of a national Church would be introduced." For the same reason, the Holy See had already turned down a petition made by the Seventh Provincial Council of Baltimore in 1849 to grant to the Archbishop of Baltimore the title and the rights of Primate of the Catholic Church in America.

It is not far-fetched to think that Rome was rather hesitant as to whether to prefer the grouping of the American Catholics by races (so as to give rise to a series of distinct churches, all under the direct control of the Holy See, as the German bishops and clergy and the Polish clergy and the clergy of other nationalities in the United States were asking for), or to favor their merging together under the rule of the Irish-American episcopate, which would make possible the gradual emergence of a homogeneous American Catholic Church. This was a new experience even for Rome, to be confronted with a Church undergoing such a rapid expansion not through conversions of the native population, but by the transplanting there of large Catholic masses from all the countries of old Europe. Some of those Roman prelates may have remembered the old Roman principle *divide et impera*, but they were fully aware that division would have created endless frictions and antagonism, and at any rate it could hardly become permanent. On the other hand, unity and homogeneity evoked before their eyes the ghost of a troublesome national church. Of course, the ideal solution was unity, a rigid Roman unity with no room for national claims or for any conspicuous distinction from other churches. And this was finally the policy adopted and applied with a strong hand by the Holy See.

In 1893 Pope Leo XIII established in Washington, D.C., an Apostolic Delegation which had been long in the offing. The Italian prelate Satolli took his residence in the American capital with authority and powers of supervision over the whole Church of the United States. Times had so changed that while in 1854 the Italian Archbishop Cajetan Bedini, who came to the States on a passing visit, was mobbed and barely escaped lynching in Cincinnati—the so-called Nativist movement being then rampant—now, on the contrary, the establishment of a permanent papal delegation in Washington caused only a few ripples in American public opinion. Perhaps those who resented it most were some disgruntled Catholic bishops.

The new Apostolic Delegate Satolli (later a Cardinal) was an angular prelate who had been a professor of medieval scholastic philosophy. He could hardly feel any sympathy with the broad modern views of Gibbons and his friends. It is permissible to suppose that his reports (as well as those of his successor Archbishop Sebastian Martinelli, an Augustinian friar), sent to the Holy See, must have confirmed and increased the fear of a growing Catholic nonconformism in America. Clouds continued to gather on the Vatican sky until the thunder burst in January 1899 with Leo's apostolic letter *Testem benevolentiae*, addressed to Cardinal Gibbons and to all American bishops, which condemned the new heresy of "Americanism."

As described by the pope, Americanism was an attempt made by well-intentioned, but misled, American clergymen to reconcile Catholic doctrine and discipline with the supposed exigencies of modern thought and modern civil liberties, at the expense of both the fundamental Catholic institutional tradition and the true character of Catholic spirituality. The pope refuted at length the American belief that active virtues, the practical virtues which express themselves in action, are more valuable and more fitting to our times than passive virtues such as had always been cherished by Catholic piety. This and other opinions which weakened the principle of authority in the Church the pope rejected not only because they were against the tradition of the Church, but also because these American novelties "create the suspicion that there are among you some who cherish the idea and wish to put up in America a Catholic Church different from that which exists in all other parts of the world." This was the most significant statement of the whole document, giving a factual definition of the purposes and aims of "Americanism."

The American bishops, dumbfounded and terrified by this blow, rushed immediately to subscribe an unconditional adhesion to the condemnation of Americanism and then looked at each other to find out who were the guilty ones. They reached the conclusion that there was really no one whose features resembled altogether the picture drawn by the pope. American Catholic historians, as a matter of fact, state that Americanism as described by the pope really did not exist in America and that all those theories which, put together, formed the dangerous heresy of Americanism had been developed in France, taking as a starting point some utterances and some ideas from American writings, but reinterpreted and developed by French clergymen in a new direction, which was not the intention of the American originals.

There is some truth in this declaration of no guilt, but neither was Pope Leo so wrong in attributing Americanism to the American bishops, or to some among them. To put it briefly, no American bishop had any intention or desire to violate any of the doctrinal or institutional principles and laws of the Church and to become a heretic or a rebel, but the views held on several questions by Gibbons, Ireland, John Joseph Keane, Martin John Spalding, and their followers, views which to their mind and according to their experience were justified and called for by the local practical exigencies and interests of the Church in the American environment, deviated in fact from those held in Rome and, if generalized as valid for the whole Church, could be, and were indeed, interpreted as leading to errors already condemned by the Holy See.

Their utterances on the advantages and the blessings that a political regime of religious freedom and separation of church and state brought to the Church, sounded very much like the theories so dear to European liberalism that the Church has nothing to fear and much to gain by the advent of political regimes based on democratic freedom. When Gibbons and Ireland praised the American system as the best for American Catholicism, they seemed to imply that this was the ideal system for the Church in the modern world, overlooking the fact that all such theories had been explicitly condemned by Gregory XVI, by Pius IX, and by Leo himself.

Much less could Pope Leo relish the emphatic insistence

of the American bishops on the American character of the Church in the United States, or such sentiments as were expressed by Ireland in addressing the Catholic Congress of 1889: "We should live in our age, know it, be in touch with it. . . . It will not do to understand the thirteenth century better than the nineteenth century. . . . The Church of America must be, of course, as Catholic as even in Jerusalem or Rome; but as far as her garments assume color from the local atmosphere, she must be American. Let no one dare paint her brow with a foreign tint, or pin to her mantle foreign linings."

It is likely that Ireland had in mind primarily the German bishops and clergy who were striving to keep their churches in America German at all cost, but his words suggested also that he thought of an American church different somehow from the rest of the Catholic Church. There was the ghost of an American national church dangling his foot over the fence.

To a pope who had imposed upon all Catholic schools the obligation to teach the scholastic philosophy of the thirteenth century, and who at all occasions stressed the point that the Church universal was first and last Roman and only Roman, Ireland's words must have caused irritation and annoyance. Last but not least, the picture of the personality and ideas of Father Isaac Thomas Hecker as drawn by his biographer, W. Elliott, and published with a preface by Ireland, could but be very distasteful to the Roman theologians. Hecker was presented as a great example of the value of active over passive virtues and of the inner working of the Spirit, in which he had so much confidence as to suggest a certain disparagement of the instrumentality of the Church in the mysterious flow of divine grace. While still a bishop of Perugia, Pope Leo had written a booklet titled *The Practice of Humility*, in which complete submission and passive obedience to the will of the ecclesiastical authority were urged as the most essential virtues of a priest. Ireland's statement in the preface to Hecker's life said that "an honest ballot and social decorum will do more for God's glory and the salvation of souls than midnight flagellation or Compostellan pilgrimages." This must have horrified the Roman theologians and prelates who conducted the trials for the canonization of saints. For much less than such revolutionary statements, Catholic writers had been summoned to appear before the Inquisition on suspicion of heretical leaning.

But Leo XIII wisely understood that all these bold utterances of the American bishops were due to American youthful exuberance, and that there was no reason to doubt the good faith, the zeal for the Church, and the attachment to the Holy See of these men. He always had a high opinion of both Gibbons and Ireland. All that was needed was a general impersonal rebuke of those novelties followed by a paternal kiss of forgiveness.

After all, the bishops and priests in America were too busy building churches to have time for theological or mystical meditations. Their activism was not the result of theoretical speculations on the nature of Catholic spirituality but a practical necessity in the bustling America of that period. The severe lesson imparted by the papal encyclical had a miraculous effect. From that time on American bishops and priests became more orthodox than any Roman prelate could be and they never again uttered a word which might have awakened the slightest suspicion or caused any irritation in the high ecclesiastical Roman spheres. The modernist movement which at the beginning of the new century created such a stir in the Catholic Church in Europe had little or no repercussion in the American Church.

The results of this historical development of the Catholic Church in democratic America during the nineteenth century were not such as the historians who have so much faith in the influence of the environment should have expected. As we have seen, this influence was felt strongly at the beginning and then again and again in the process of growth of American Catholicism, giving rise to a vague vision of an American Catholic Church that would reflect at least in part the American spirit, or, in Ireland's words, a Church having a distinct American tint and wearing American garments.

But in the modern Catholic Church there is no longer any room for what were once called national churches forming one church but each distinct from the other by local traditions, customs, and special institutions going back to ancient or medieval times. The totalitarian Roman ecclesiastical system has attained in modern times its full historical realization and is now able to enforce uniformity under the absolute rule of a highly centralized papal government. And just because Catholicism in America, transplanted here in a land of democratic freedom, had no national traditions of its own, and had no entanglements with political institutions and interests, but had to depend upon its own spiritual and material resources, it lent itself more easily to the process of being molded into the rigid pattern of Roman totalitarianism.

4

THE TWENTIETH CENTURY

THE CHURCH ON THE OFFENSIVE

By the Apostolic Constitution *Sapienti consilio* of Pius X (June 29, 1908), the Catholic Church in America ceased to be a church of missions under the special jurisdiction of the Congregation *de Propaganda Fide*, and became a full-fledged member of the great Catholic ecclesiastical organization. It was now submitted to all the general rules and prescriptions of Canon Law and to the regulations of the various departments of the central government of the Church in Rome. The American Church had come of age. The ten years since the condemnation of the heresy of Americanism had shown that it was cured of its juvenile overconfidence in its own spirit. It was time to bestow on American Catholicism the badge of maturity.

This change in its juridical status did not cause any considerable modification of the outward structure and the internal discipline of the American Church. Not a few of the

Tridentine rules had already been introduced, and many new papal laws and prescriptions had been applied also to the church in America. Moreover, the special form of diocesan organization and government, with no canonically instituted parishes, no ecclesiastical benefices, and a strict concentration of powers in episcopal hands was preserved almost intact. In general, however, the end of the missionary regime, which in the Catholic church marks only a temporary stage, gave to the American Church a new strong feeling of permanence and stability and a normal place in the whole Catholic system.

This period also marks a turning point in the history of American Catholicism for another reason. The Catholic Church in America from its very beginning had been forced to assume, and to remain for a long time, in a defensive position. Representing a small minority of the population, with many foreign elements not yet assimilated, Catholicism faced a widely spread sense of hostility which flared up periodically, kindled by the common belief that it was a body foreign to American traditions. The Church, therefore, had concentrated its efforts in resisting the attacks and in trying to dispel the notion that it was a foreign institution with no right to be and to call itself American. But now the situation was changing fast.

The Church had weathered well the last assault at the ramparts of Catholicism by the so-called American Protective Association of the early 1890s; its numerical strength had reached the considerable figure of about 10 million members; its high clergy were now mostly native American; among its laity not few held high offices in the public

administration of the federal, state, and municipal governments and in the administration of justice, while many
more had acquired wealth, and some of them even had
climbed high on the economic ladder. A century of experience had shown that, after all, Catholics could be, and most
of them were, in fact, good and solid American citizens. The
time had come for the Church to come out of the trenches
and to take the offensive in the great undertaking of con-
quering the United States to the Catholic faith, for the salvation of the souls, for the greater happiness of the country,
and for the glory of God. The vitality of a church manifests
itself in its missionary spirit and achievements, and American Catholicism had plenty of youthful vitality.

The First World War, and then the U.S. laws restricting
immigration which checked the too rapid increase of the
foreign Catholic population, gave to the Church a respite
from the exacting task of making, in haste, provisions for
their spiritual needs. This task absorbed for a long time a
large part of its energies and its resources, but now it was
possible to gather and concentrate all available forces on a
well-planned program of Catholic expansion. The same war
gave also to the Church the opportunity of establishing a
new organization, the Catholic War Council, with its headquarters in Washington. Unity and uniformity in the ecclesiastical regime of the Church had been secured first by the
legislation of the American Synods, then by the institution
of the Apostolic Delegation, and finally by the end of the
missionary period. But Catholic activities and propaganda
in the social, economic, and political fields were still left to
the local initiative and judgment of each bishop in his own

territory and according to his views. Conflicts of opinions resulting in contradictory measures and tactics had caused no little troubles. Unpleasant incidents, such as mutual denunciations to Rome, had taken place when the reactionary section of the episcopate tried to stop by all means the new trend represented by the more progressive elements in the hierarchy such as Gibbons and Ireland.

The Catholic War Council, established to handle the problems created by the war as they affected the Catholic Church in the United States, was so successful and demonstrated so clearly the advantages of a central organization directing and coordinating all Catholic forces in a common action, that when the war was over, the institution was made permanent. It changed its name to that of Catholic Welfare Council and, later on, to that of National Catholic Welfare Conference, setting aside the word "Council." which smacked too much of an ecclesiastical organ. Its basis of action was enlarged, its programs were developed and perfected to cover the whole range of American life. The Catholic Welfare Conference is now a complex and powerful machine through which Catholic action reaches all the vital organs and institutions of the nation, from the departments of government and from Congress in Washington to the last municipal administration in the country, and all classes, from the great industrial and banking lords to the workers in factories and the farmers in the rural regions of the United States.

It would be impossible even to summarize here all the great gains made by Catholicism in America during the years between the First and the Second World Wars and during these last years of the 1940s. It will suffice to mention the growth in numbers of Catholic dioceses, of Catholic schools, colleges, and universities; the formation or further development of hundreds of associations of Catholic professionals and tradesmen, of women and children and people in all walks of life, which perpetuate an impressive religious sectionalism going from the guild of Catholic judges and lawyers to those of street cleaners and cab drivers; the expansion and strict regimentation of the Catholic press which shapes Catholic opinion in each Catholic diocese; the growth of ecclesiastical wealth by the acquisition of large estates, investments, and gifts and the creation of special funds for various purposes; the first attempt in the political field to send a Catholic to the White House; the actual control by Catholics of the public administration of several states and of many large cities; the election of a sizable group of Catholic representatives and senators to Congress, and the growth of the political influence of the Catholic hierarchy on the federal government, which reached its climax in the establishment of the presidential embassy to the Vatican.

This embassy, as we learn from the correspondence of President Franklin D. Roosevelt and Pope Pius XII, had the purpose of coordinating the activities of the United States and of the Vatican for the reestablishment of peace, for the relief of the sufferings inflicted to the peoples by the war, and for the work of material and moral reconstruction to be done when the war was over. But to these another utilitarian reason was added by Catholic and non-Catholic newspapers to justify, in the eyes of American public opinion, the unusual step taken by President Roosevelt. The Vatican, they said, is the best observatory in the world to know what is happening anytime and everywhere in all countries. By having there an ambassador of the president, the United States government was able to get very valuable information which helped in the conduct of the war and is now helping in the establishment of peace. This explanation, which has become classic in Catholic rebuttals of Protestant denunciations of the embassy, implies that the Vatican, which had declared its absolute neutrality, was willing during the war to put at the disposal of the United States its wide service of information, making thus a dent in its neutrality unless the same information was made available also to the other side. We may be sure that as long as the fate of the war hung in the balance, the Vatican was not ready to make such a blunder as to break its neutrality, and that neither was it disposed to become a clearinghouse of information for all belligerent nations. But so long as this naive explanation satisfies American public opinion, the Vatican, being anxious that the embassy be preserved and eventually be made permanent, has not cared to issue any denial of these statements, though they are not flattering to the usually meticulous correctness of its diplomacy.

Having gained so much ground and having conquered important strategic positions along the whole line and in all sectors of American life, the Catholic hierarchy in its march forward to make the United States a Catholic country, took a new and far-reaching step. On November 20, 1948, the committee of bishops forming the board of the National Catholic Welfare Conference issued a long statement under the title "The Christian in Action." This statement, signed by four cardinals, five archbishops, and five bishops, representing the whole Catholic hierarchy of the United States, is not an expression of private opinions, but an official pronouncement of the American Catholic Church.

The whole document purports to be a denunciation of the heresy of "secularism" and a prescription to cure this disease which afflicts the soul of the American nation. The episcopal statement covers a wide field: It deals briefly with religion in the home, religion in education, religion in economic life, and then at great length with religion and citizenship, or, to put it in plain language, religion and the American political system insofar as it affects the church. This is the new and essential part of the whole document, the rest is merely a restatement of old positions made here for the sake of completeness.

The bishops were moved to issue this statement primarily by the decision of the Supreme Court of the United States in *McCollum* v. *Champaign Board of Education* (March 1948), in which the imparting of religious instruction in a public school was declared to be forbidden by the Constitution of the United States. The bishops denounced this decision as being itself unconstitutional and a very dangerous step toward the transformation of the United States into a totalitarian state on the pattern of Moscow. Two main questions are thus raised by the episcopal statement: one is that of religious instruction in public schools, the other is that of the separation of church and state in the American Constitution.

As for the schools, only a few points need be mentioned.

At the time when the American Constitution was written, there were no public schools; the only schools in existence were those kept and supported by religious denominations or private groups. By and by the various states of the Union disestablished their churches; the system of public schools began to grow and the denominational schools began to disappear. Since schools and education were a concern of the individual states and of cities and towns, the establishment and growth of public schools, far from being uniform, was marked by a great variety of programs, standards, and policies. Soon a great controversy began as to what kind of religious instruction could and should be given in those schools. The problem in most communities, having at that time almost entirely Protestant populations, was that of finding a kind of common denominator in religious instruction which could be acceptable to all the competing and quarreling Protestant churches. To put an end to this controversy, the religious instruction to be given in the public schools was finally reduced in most communities to the reading of some passages from the Bible and the singing of some religious hymns. It was at this point that the Catholics entered the fray.

According to Catholic doctrine the right and duty to educate children belongs first to the family. This does not mean that the family is free to choose any religion. Like the individual and the community, the family has the obligation to teach the only true religion, that is, the Catholic religion. But since the family nowadays, for various reasons, is not able or does not care to perform this function, this duty devolves by a kind of tacit delegation of the parents and by divine right to the Church which comes next in line. By divine institution, the Church has not only the exclusive right to impart religious instruction, but also to direct and supervise the whole educational process, to make sure that nothing is taught contrary to faith and morals. Finally, at the end comes the state, which as such has no right or competence to teach anything, but has only the duty to provide the means needed by the family and the Church to perform their educational task. Of course, the right of the state to exercise a certain external control in the matter of organization and administration of schools is admitted, but the supreme control and the responsibility must be left exclusively to the Church. In other words, the Catholic Church claims a monopoly on education and schools.

To advance this claim in an almost solid Protestant country, as the United States was at that time, was, of course, out of the question. The Catholic Church very early established some schools or colleges for boys, aiming above all to recruit candidates for the priesthood; but Catholic children had no other alternative but that of attending the public schools. The practice followed in those schools of reading the Bible in the Protestant version and of singing hymns from the repertoire of Protestant churches was strongly objected to by the Catholic hierarchy. The Fourth Provincial Council of Baltimore in 1840 instructed the pastors of all Catholic parishes to see to it that Catholic children attending public schools did not use the Protestant version of the Bible or sing sectarian hymns. The pastors were also enjoined to employ their influence with local school boards to prevent the introduction of such practices into the public schools.

It was obvious that the Protestant majority would never discard the reading of the Protestant version in favor of the Catholic version. After all, if the reading of the Protestant version was "sectarian," the same charge could be leveled against the reading of the Catholic version, and still more against the reading of both of them. The Catholic hierarchy had meanwhile begun to establish parochial schools of its own in some large centers of Catholic population. A few years later, in 1852, the First Plenary Council of Baltimore exhorted the bishops to build a school in every parish to be supported by parochial funds. The same exhortation was repeated by the Second Plenary Council in 1866, adding also that, for Catholic children attending public schools, classes in catechism should be instituted in each parish. The Third and last Plenary Council of Baltimore, in 1884, imposed on all pastors of Catholic parishes the strict obligation to establish within two years a parochial school, and on all Catholic parents that of sending their children to such schools, unless they received a dispensation from the bishop.

The sharp controversy about the Bible in public schools went on for some time until most school boards suppressed the reading of it and the singing of religious hymns in the program of their public schools.

But soon afterward both Catholic and Protestant leaders began to deplore the fact that no religious instruction at all was imparted in public schools. This was a moral disaster for which, according to the Catholics, the responsibility was to be laid at the door of the Protestants and their sectarian intolerance, and, vice versa, according to the Protestants, was to be charged altogether to the narrow-minded selfishness of the Catholics. Both assigned at least part of the blame also to the Jews.

The task of building up a whole system of parochial schools was a formidable one, and the burden went on increasing when the Catholic immigration became more intense in the last decades of the nineteenth century. Whereupon some bishops, and especially Archbishop Ireland of St. Paul, began to work on compromises with local school boards by which parochial schools could be taken in within the public school system and be supported by public funds, or merge with the public schools on condition that religious denominational instruction could be imparted in the school buildings in after school hours.

These plans were put into experiment (the Poughkeepsie system and the Faribault system) in spite of strong opposition from Protestant groups. Strange to say, a section of the Catholic episcopate did not look with favor upon them either, because, though the school boards paid rent for the use of the parochial school buildings and paid salaries to the nun teachers, some bishops did not think that the faith of Catholic children was protected enough by the arrangement.

The case was taken to Rome and the Holy See decided that these experiments could be tolerated because the Church was not hostile to public schools provided some objectionable features in them be removed. In fact, however, these various arrangements made with local school boards did not prove in the end to be satisfactory to either side. Even now, other similar experiments, in a modified form, are still carried on in many cities and towns of several states. Probably most of them, if not all, would be rejected as unconstitutional by the Supreme Court if recourse should ever be made to its judgment.

From the point of view of the Catholic Church, these precarious and only local arrangements, the existence and continuation of which depends upon the good will of local school boards whose personnel often changes at each new election, do not solve the problem. The only satisfactory solution is that of the Catholic schools.

There are in the United States today (1949) about 10,000 parochial schools with an attendance of about 3 million children (a little over 50 percent of all the Catholic children in the country), and a teaching staff of about 80,000 nuns. There are also about 1,600 Catholic high schools and over 200 colleges and universities. All these schools are under the direct and complete control of the clergy. Their cost is kept at a low level by the fact that nun teachers and members of religious orders, who own most of the colleges, receive no regular salaries. Even so the total cost to be met by fees paid by the students and by contributions from Catholic families is a very heavy burden which becomes heavier from year to year with the addition of new schools and the improvements needed by the old ones. At the same time, it seems that the recruitment of nun teachers, indispensable to keep the system alive, is far from meeting the needs, and according to Catholic sources, is becoming more and more difficult with the present young generation.

Confronted with this situation, the Catholic hierarchy has decided that the time has come to force once and for all a radical solution to the problem. This solution was suggested by Pope Pius XII. According to the pope, the only school that the Catholic Church could approve of would be one where Catholics are free to follow their own system of teaching in schools entirely Catholic. In these schools, however, religious instruction would be provided for non-Catholics according to legitimate demand of parents. Financial support from public funds should be given to all such schools that meet with the reasonable demands of the state.

The path to this solution is blocked by the system of public schools and by the separation of church and state. Catholic strategy is, therefore, directed against these two obstacles which must be removed to reach the goal. The attack against public schools by the Catholic hierarchy is based on two assumptions: first, that a school with no religious instruction is a godless school, is immoral, and hence it trains bad citizens, atheists, and criminals; the second is that such a school is un-American and contrary to the ideas and intentions of the founders of the American republic. The attack against the separation of church and state is likewise based on the assumption that this separation, as understood by the Supreme Court of the United States, is not to be found at all in the Constitution but is a product of modern secularism.

Before resorting to this direct attack, the hierarchy had tried indirect ways of breaking down, step by step, the wall which prevented any direct contribution by the public treasury to Catholic schools. During these last years, Catholics were successful in obtaining in several cities bus service at public expense for the transportation of pupils of parochial schools. Catholic hopes rose very high when the Supreme Court, in *Everson* v. *Board of Education of Ewing Township,*

New Jersey (February 1947), decided by a vote of five to four that the grant of this benefit made to children, and not directly to parochial schools, was not forbidden by the Constitution of the United States. In announcing this decision, however, the Court warned that the principle of separation of church and state remained firm in the American law and constitutional tradition. As a matter of fact, a year later, in the *McCollum* case of 1948, *People of the State of Illinois, ex rel.* (*McCollum* v. *Board of Education*), the Supreme Court by a vote of eight to one decided that to impart religious instruction in a public school is forbidden by the Constitution, and reaffirmed the principle of separation of church and state without compromise, thus shutting the door to further concessions.

The indignation of the Catholic hierarchy was voiced by several bishops, especially against Justice Frank Murphy, who though a Catholic, concurred in the decision of the majority. "I wonder how a Catholic could do such a thing," remarked Archbishop Richard Cushing of Boston in a public speech. The episcopal reaction to the decision of the Court found full expression in the November statement which must be set against this background to understand its full meaning.

"Secularism," the bishops state, "that is, the failure to center life in God, creator of men, is a deadly menace to our Christian and American way of life." After denouncing briefly the various manifestations of this secularism in American life, the bishops come to the central point of the statement, which may be condensed as follows:

Secularism, in the sense explained above, is a rather recent development in the United States. It did not exist, or at least, it had little or no importance, at the beginning of our national life. Today it is rampant, and it has found a most poisonous instrument in the exclusion of religion from public education and in the separation of church and state. Neither of these two things is American. From the beginning, religion was set at the basis of American life. The true American tradition concerning the place of religion in our political life is shown by the Northwest Ordinance passed by Congress in 1787, reenacted in 1790, and adopted by the constitutions of several states, which enjoins, "Religion, morality and knowledge, being necessary to good citizenship and the happiness of mankind, schools and the means of education shall forever be encouraged."

The American system of law was also founded on the religious notion that man, as a creature of God, is bound to observe God's moral law. God is at the beginning and at the end of all laws by which the government exercises control over its citizens for the common good. This is the American philosophy of law. The Constitution in its First Amendment does not even mention the separation of church and state. It says only that Congress shall not have the power of making laws "respecting an establishment of religion or prohibiting the free exercise thereof." In view of the place which the founders of the American republic assigned to religion as a necessary factor for the

happiness of the citizens, as shown by the Northwest Ordinance, it is clear that, though for practical and valuable reasons they forbade the establishment of any religion as the official religion of
the republic, they had no intention of separating
the church from the state in the meaning of the
Supreme Court. On the contrary, what they
wanted was the cooperation of church and state
for the protection and advancement of religion.
Let us then go back to the true American tradition.
Of course, in a country of divided religious allegiance, the cooperation of church and state should
not create inequalities; this cooperation should be
with all the churches without granting special
privileges to any of them to the exclusion of the
others. Religious education is the main field in
which this cooperation is most needed, and since
the state has the obligation to supply the material
means for the education of our children and our
youth, the schools kept by religious denominations have the right to request and to be granted
financial help by the state. The decision of the
Supreme Court in the *McCollum* case is against
logic and against history; it conflicts with the law
and with the intentions of the framers of the Constitution. We, the bishops state, have no desire to
introduce novelties or to change our American
Constitution. Far from it, we raise our voice to
insist on its observance. It is the Supreme Court
that has introduced innovations and has betrayed
the spirit and the letter of the Constitution. It is
the Supreme Court that, by sanctioning secu-

larism, is leading the United States's system of laws toward the ideas and practices of the "omnipotent state" which would transform our democratic institutions into totalitarian institutions.

The statement ends with a vigorous appeal to American Catholics to carry on a relentless campaign to bring about a reversal of the Supreme Court's decision and to reestablish in this country the original system of cooperation of church and state.

Leaving to competent jurists the task of analyzing the technical aspect of the constitutional problem, I will make only a few remarks from the historical angle of the question. First of all, however, we must remember that the Catholic bishops, like all other American citizens, have the right freely to express their opinion, to criticize and protest against the finding of the Supreme Court, which is not infallible. Likewise, they have the right to use all legitimate means to make their opinion prevail and to carry on an agitation for the reversal of that decision or for passing a new amendment to the constitution, and, last but not least, they are acting for the interest of their Church according to its doctrinal, its normative principles. There is nothing secret or sinister in their designs: Their aim is to conquer gradually the whole population to the true faith, the Catholic faith, to save millions of American souls. They cherish the vision in the far-away future of a nation of 200 million Catholics with 2,000 bishops who by that time may rule the whole Church of God.

In the episcopal statement, the term "secularism" is used as being equivalent to theoretical or practical atheism. But the historical and political connotations of secularism do not justify this identification. To understand its meaning, we must notice that the opposite of secularism is clericalism or confessionalism, the names of a political system which advocates the union of church and state and the subordination of many activities of the state to those of the church, and the consequent predominance of the ecclesiastical class in the whole life of the nation. Secularism (the English equivalent of *laicismus*) is the name of a political system which rejects this union of church and state in the name of freedom of conscience and of religion, assumes a neutral attitude toward all religions because the alternative would be religious discrimination, intolerance, and persecution, and does not admit that the clergy as a class should dictate government policies. As such, the secular state is not necessarily either atheist or irreligious. Far from it, the modern secular democratic state grants freedom and protection to all religions, that is, to the worship of God according to the various faiths, and does not interfere with their religious and moral teaching. In such a state, a law that would impose the obligation of teaching atheism in the schools would be unconstitutional, just as much as any law that would establish a church. The episcopal statement has overlooked the fundamental distinction between secularism as a political system and secularism as an ideological system, as a general vision of life which discards religion altogether. Of course, from the totalitarian standpoint of the Catholic Church, such a distinction is theoretically wrong, just as it is wrong from the standpoint of totalitarian communism. In both the Catholic and the communist totalitarian ideologies, secu-

larism is identified with atheism, to be condemned and exe-
crated by the former, and, on the contrary, to be set at the
basis of life by the latter.

This, however, does not mean that the notion of political
secularism is either illogical or inconsistent with moral and
religious principles. It means only that this notion starts
from democratic antitotalitarian premises which allow a
distinction between political and ideological secularism as
well as between Catholicism (a religious system) and clericalism (a political system). Political secularism is not the
result of theological theories, but is the practical and logical
application of a higher and more universal ethical principle,
which is the recognition and respect of the right of individual conscience not to be coerced to accept a religious
faith or to practice a specific faith, a principle which after all,
is admitted by the same Catholic tradition.

As a matter of fact, apart from Russia, at least with
respect to the reestablishment of the Orthodox Church and
while atheism was officially taught in its schools, the only
two other states whose ideologies, in the judgment of Pope
Pius XII, were altogether pagan and antireligious were the
Fascist and the Nazi totalitarian states. Strange as it may
seem, both of them, by making concordats with the Holy
See, wished to appear as having discarded political secularism, and one of them, the Fascist state, appeared to have
become virtually a confessional Catholic state.

Another word which in the episcopal statement is used
with a special meaning is the word "Christian." The word
"Catholic" seldom appears in its lines (and only in such connections as "Catholic youth" or "Catholic parents" or

"Catholic people"), while the more general word "Christian" is always used in such phrases as "Christian vision of life," "Christian moral principles," "Christian thought and action," and so on. A few times the word "Christian" is used specifically for non-Catholics, as in the following passage: "There is only one truth indivisible, and those Christians who think that they can pick and choose from it may hold themselves to be Christians and are accepted as Christians, but they have never been thrilled by the glory of the truth of Christ in action."

Obviously the indivisible truth is the Catholic truth, and those who pick and choose and call themselves Christians are the Protestants (this word never appears in the document). They, say the bishops, "criticize and even deplore the decay of morality and the spread of corruption in public life, but they feel no obligation to do anything about it." Having thus rebuked those Protestant Christians who remain passive while religion is disintegrating, the Catholic hierarchy assumes the right to speak in the name of all Christianity. The constant and intentional use of the word "Christian," avoiding the specific term "Catholic," intends to convey the idea that the cause for which the Catholic Church is fighting is a cause common to all Christians of all denominations and sects and that all good Protestants who still care for religious education and morality should join the Catholic forces for the defeat of secularism and the revival of religious life in America.

There is no doubt that most Americans of all religious faiths would agree with the statement that religion must have a place in the process of education of children and youth. They would agree also that there is a sound American religious tradition which from the beginning of the republic has given a Christian character to American institutions. But we may be sure that few, if any, American non-Catholics would agree with the bishops' denunciation of political secularism as being un-American, and much less would approve of the concrete aims which the hierarchy wishes to attain in this new campaign.

The real problem with which we are confronted is that of how, when, and by whom religious education can be imparted in the United States, a country where there is no established religion, where there are widely divergent religious beliefs and churches, all of them having equal rights before the law in a democratic regime that guarantees to all citizens freedom of conscience, of religion, of speech, and of assembly. According to the Catholic hierarchy, the public school is the place where religious education should be given. According to the American Constitution as interpreted by the Supreme Court, the public school is not the place for it. This decision of the Supreme Court is criticized by the episcopal statement as a repudiation by the Court of religious education in principle and as an evidence that the Court is pursuing an atheist policy and a policy of statolatry similar to that of the totalitarian states, and of Moscow in particular. It is rather difficult to believe that such ideas, intentions, and aims could be attributed to the Supreme Court, which in the same *McCollum* case added to the decision the following statement: "To hold that a state cannot consistently with the constitution utilize its public schools to aid any or all religious faiths or sects in the dissemination of their doctrine and ideals ... does not manifest a governmental hostility to religion or religious teaching. A manifestation of such hostility would be at war with our national tradition . . . which guarantees the free exercise of religion. For, the first amendment rests upon the premise that both religion and government can best work to achieve their lofty aims if each is left free from the other within its respective sphere."

Ignoring this fundamental point so clearly stated by the Court, the bishops, who refuse to distinguish between ideological secularism and political secularism, identify once more the two distinct questions, that of religious education in general and that of religious education in public schools. But why, from the Catholic point of view, is it essential that religious instruction should be given in public schools and not elsewhere? The reason is neither because there are no alternatives nor because the churches are not free to impart religious instruction in any other way or places as they please. The main reason as stated by Catholic authorities is twofold: One is that religious instruction must integrate the whole educational process and must be imparted together with the rest of knowledge so as to build the moral character of the children; the other is that it is very difficult for the Church to get hold of children elsewhere than the school. Both these reasons have only a relative and not an absolute value; they are reasons of convenience and not of necessity. The integration of secular and religious instruction can be well achieved in special religious classes provided by the Church. As for the difficulty of getting the children together, that is a matter which concerns only the zeal and the efficiency of the individual churches and not the state or the police. Religious instruction is the task of the Church, and a difficult task it is. But the Catholic Church has, up to now, performed it without interfering with the public schools by establishing classes of catechism and religious instruction in the church for pupils of public schools, and then by building up its own system of parochial schools, as the easiest, though more costly, way of serving the interests of the Church.

In comparison to the difficulties now experienced by the Church, those which would face the state by letting religion play havoc with the public schools are much greater, apart from the question of the Constitution. Even if all the Christian Churches in the United States should agree to permit religious instruction on a few points accepted by all, such as the existence of God and of a moral law of universal value, this teaching would not escape the connotation of being sectarian, because it would be more or less a diluted form of Unitarianism.

As a matter of fact, the aim of the Catholic hierarchy is not the introduction of some form of religious instruction in public schools. They know that it cannot be done without causing inequalities in the treatment of religions. The plan which they advocate is that of supplanting the system of public schools by a system of denominational schools supported by the state. The adoption of this plan would bring about a paradoxical situation. There are in the United States over 230 religious denominations and bodies, and each of them would be entitled to put up schools supported by the public treasury. There can be no doubt that most of them would avail themselves of this privilege and would be eager to have a complete set of schools of their own, from elementary schools to colleges and universities. And why should not atheists and unbelievers forming associations ask also for schools at the expense of the state? We may be sure that this is the last thing that the Catholic hierarchy would like to see happen in this country. What they may have in mind is a system in which the privilege of being supported by the state would be restricted to denominational schools already in existence or to be built up by the denominations at their own expense and meeting exacting requirements in matters of numbers of pupils and equipment. Such a system would secure to the Catholic Church, which has already a large and well-organized system of schools, a unique advantage over all Protestant churches, while the smaller denominations which would never be able to meet these qualifications would be automatically eliminated. But this plan, which would introduce discriminations, and other similar plans which may be devised, meet now with the formidable obstacle of being forbidden by the Constitution as interpreted by the Supreme Court.

This is the core of the problem. From the standpoint of the episcopal statement, the provision of the First Amendment forbidding an establishment of religion, when set against its historical background, means nothing more than making unlawful any legislative act granting a monopoly of state favors to one particular religion. But there is nothing in it which suggests that it forbade the federal government to maintain relations with various forms of religion or even support them, provided it did not discriminate among them. The separation of church and state as now understood simply did not exist at that time, while a system of cooperation of the state with religion was widely practiced in most of the states of the union. This is the Catholic contention.

It would be preposterous and unhistorical to attribute to

the framers of the American Constitution ideas and notions of separation of church and state which belong to a later period and were suggested by new circumstances and new experiments. The framers of the Constitution, whatever their personal religious convictions and their ideas about the function of religion may have been, were confronted with a practical twofold problem: how to secure religious freedom for all, and how to avoid, in this regime of freedom, any religious-political conflict between church and state and among the various religions themselves. They solved the problem by forbidding religious discriminations in the exercise of civic rights and by forbidding the establishment of a religion, while granting to all of them complete freedom to exist and to make propaganda.

We must not forget that this was the first experiment on a large national scale ever made, up to that time, of a state with no established church. The establishment of a church was not an abstract notion; it was a concrete legal institution very well known to the framers of the Constitution because it had existed in the colonies and was still in existence in several of the original states of the Union. They knew that the establishment of a religion meant first that the official state church was a public institution with special rights and privileges not shared by any other religion or church which usually were forbidden to exist within the state. In the second place it meant that the official church had the monopoly of education in the state and the control through censorship of the intellectual life of the country. Last but not least, it meant that the official church had the right to be supported by the state either by exacting special taxes or in some other way.

It is a logical inference that the framers of the Constitution, by forbidding the establishment of a church, intended to forbid the grant of religious monopoly and educational monopoly, as well as the grant of state financial support to any religion or church. As a matter of fact, the disestablished churches lost their juridical status of public institutions under the *ius publicum* (public law) and sank down to the same level with all other churches, becoming merely private associations and organizations, or corporations of citizens having a religious purpose, registered as such according to the laws and regulations of the state. As a result, churches as such have no juridical personality and legal existence; what, in the eyes of the law, do exist are the individual corporations such as the corporation of the Catholic Church in Massachusetts, in New York, in Chicago, and so on. This change in the juridical status of the churches brought about by the disestablishment and the prohibition to establish a church must not be overlooked.

It seems obvious that the purpose of the First Amendment was the cutting, once and for all, of the religious, political, educational, and economic ties which bound the state to the church in the old regime of the union of church and state with an established church. No one contests that freedom of religion and of religious education and the equality of all religions before the law are clearly implied in the First Amendment, but objections are raised against the inclusion in the prohibition to establish a religion also the prohibition of the last implication concerning financial aid to or support of churches and their institutions by the state, and especially of church denominational schools.

Though the First Amendment is silent on this point, according to this view, it was not the intention of the lawgivers to forbid such financial aid, and the text of the amendment adopted by them, and as we have it, does not include this prohibition. Some historical evidence is brought in favor of this thesis.

In the debate in Congress which preceded the adoption of this text, the representatives of the state of Virginia objected to it just because it did not contain a clause which they wanted, forbidding in so many words financial subsidies to religious bodies, while their opponents approved of the text for the same reason, that it did not contain such a clause, because they were not against the granting of those subsidies. In conclusion, both sides, though for opposite reasons, thought that the proposed text of the law did not contain, at least not necessarily, the prohibition of material aid to religion by the federal government. This argument, from the intention of the lawgivers as presented, seems to be clear enough.

The acceptance of this evidence does not, however, solve the question because the facts so stated may be approached from a different angle. It is obvious that, as far as the essential question of whether material aid to religions should or should not be permitted was concerned, opinions in Congress (the lawgiver) were divided; some were against granting such aid, and some were not against it. From this point of view, the intention of the lawgiver was neutralized by the dissention.

The question is then restricted to the text, to the words of the law (constitutional amendment). On this point, some members of Congress thought that an explicit clause forbidding material aid to religion should be included; others, on the contrary, thought that no such clause should be inserted. It is to be noticed that these opponents to the insertion of that clause did not propose to insert in the text of the law a clause permitting or making obligatory the grant of material aid to religion. Finally, the majority of Congress adopted the proposed text in its naked absolute form: "Congress shall make no laws respecting the establishment of a religion," adding no qualifications, exemptions, or exceptions whatsoever.

Is it logical to conclude from this evidence that, in passing this law (constitutional amendment), the intention of Congress was that of forbidding only an unequal treatment of religions in dispensing the favors of the government, and not of forbidding any material aid to religion? The method of juridical exegesis by which this conclusion is reached is at least questionable.

The intention of the lawgiver is a fundamental canon in jurisprudence, but no less fundamental is the principle that *Lex quod voluit expressit, quod noluit tacuit* (laws express what they want and what they do not want they pass under silence), and this principle is rigidly applied, especially in matters inducing obligations or granting privileges and exemptions. The divergent opinions expressed in the debate of the law and of its text do not change the fact that the law which was passed is what it is. The intention of the lawgiver cannot put in the text of the law what is not there, or eliminate from it what is there, without saying so in a clear and unmistakable provision added to the text. This principle is stressed in both civil and canon law: The intention of the lawgiver must be *aliquo modo saltem in fomula legis expressa*; otherwise *nihil operatur* (the intention of the lawgiver must be at least in some way expressed in the words [formula] of the law, otherwise it has no effect).

In the case of the First Amendment, these points are out of the question:

1. That the historical and juridical notion of an established church held at that time and known to the legislator included the obligation of the state to give financial support to the established religion; and, vice versa, the disestablishment of a religion and the prohibition to establish a religion implied also a prohibition to give such support. This support was an integral and essential part of the notion of an established religion; to grant this support, while forbidding the establishment of a religion, would destroy and nullify the general prohibition itself because a religion supported by the state is at least in part an established religion.

2. The text of the law (amendment) as passed and as we have it is silent on this point; it does not grant, and it does not forbid, material aid to religion by the state. The inference that can be derived from this silence is that the Virginians were wrong in thinking that the prohibition to support a religion was not in the text of the law, but their opponents were still more wrong if they thought that the text permitted that support. No clause forbidding it was needed because the prohibition to establish a religion was absolute and carried with it all its implications, while, on the contrary, a clause permitting it, in derogation of the law, would have been essential and had to be explicit in its words and in its meaning. *Intentio mente retenta nihil operatur.*

Neither does the fact that, for a long time in some states, connections and dealings with local churches continued to affect in any way the principle of the First Amendment. As is well known, the text of this amendment which forbids the establishment of a church was followed immediately by the provision that the states of the Union were free to have an established church if they wanted it, and to do in this matter whatever they pleased. This contradictory provision, which nullified in practice the preceding section so far as some old states of the Union were concerned, was the price which the federal Constitution had to pay to be acceptable to those states so jealous of their sovereign right to legislate even on religious matters. In fact, the First Amendment marked the goal to be reached by and by that the old states disestablish their churches, while the new states gradually added to the Union had to conform in a general way to the federal statutes.

It took some time before the principle of the First Amendment won general recognition in the American dual system of federal and state sovereignty, and still a longer time before all its implications were unfolded with the rise of new situations. Practices inconsistent with the First Amendment can be found at times in various states, but to assume that these practices represent the true American legal tradition and are evidence of the meaning then attributed to the First Amendment, is, to say the least, a very strange historical procedure. A more positive indication of what this legal tradition was is to be found in the fact that most states of the Union, beginning with Connecticut in 1818, as soon as the system of public schools began to be built up, introduced in their constitutions an explicit provision forbidding the grant of any money from the public treasury to any but the public school.

Unconstitutional practices occur even now, and they may go on undisturbed for a long time, because in the American system these matters are solved by the courts and, finally, by the Supreme Court which is the official interpreter of the Constitution. But the Supreme Court being a judiciary and not a legislative body, has no right of initiative and has to wait for specific cases to be submitted to its jurisdiction. As a matter of fact, only in recent times have important cases involving these aspects of the First Amendment, which we are here discussing, been submitted to the Supreme Court. The law passed by the state of Oregon imposing on all parents the obligation to send their children only to public schools was declared unconstitutional, because freedom of education, though not mentioned in the Constitution, is a logical implication of freedom of thought and of religion. The principle forbidding the establishment of a religion makes unlawful the grant of a monopoly of education to any church, and likewise the principle of religious freedom makes unlawful the usurpation by the state of a monopoly of schools and educational institutions.

The decision of the Supreme Court in the *McCollum* case is also founded on the logical and historical implications of the First Amendment which, in the Court's judgment, forbids the state to give material aid to any or all religious faiths in the dissemination of their doctrines and ideals. If the opposite principle were admitted, and the interpretation suggested by the episcopal statement accepted, that the First Amendment forbids only any discrimination among the various religions in the grant of this aid, the logical conclusion would be that the First Amendment forbids the establishment of one religion, but permits and is duty bound to bring about the partial establishment of all religions, a paradoxical conclusion so absurd as to be inconceivable.

The phrase, "separation of church and state," is very objectionable to the Catholic Church. It has been condemned again and again by the Holy See. When adopted by some Catholic countries of Europe, this separation meant the disestablishment of the Catholic Church, the loss of all its privileges and monopolies, the confiscation of ecclesiastical possessions, and even the enactment of laws restricting the common and constitutional liberties of the Catholic Church. It was a hostile and undemocratic system of separation. But the American system of separation—whether it is called by this or by any other name is immaterial—has not, and never had, this connotation of hostility. It has been called, even by the recent popes, a system of friendly separation, in which religious rights and liberties are protected by the law, with no discrimination and no interference by the state in the sphere of religious action.

The American separation, as expressed in the First Amendment, affected unfavorably the Protestant denominations which were disestablished, but it was voted by a Congress almost entirely composed of Protestant members, and it was cheerfully accepted by most Protestant churches. For the Catholic Church, it was a boon. It was highly praised and appreciated by the Catholic clergy and by all who began to experience the benefits of liberty. Devotion to American institutions, including this kind of American separation of church and state, was urged upon all Catholics by the ecclesiastical hierarchy. It was advocated by Cardinal Gibbons as one of the necessary qualifications of a native American clergy.

Of course Gibbons and the Catholic bishops knew well that the principle and practice of separation was condemned by their church, but they did not think that this condemnation applied to the friendly and not hostile separation sanctioned by American laws, or at least they acted as if this was their belief. It was only in recent times, and after Leo XIII's condemnation of Americanism, that the American hierarchy and the clergy increasingly began to show a keen awareness of the evils of the American separation of church and state. It was during the controversy on the establishment of the presidential embassy to the Vatican that Cardinal Frances Joseph Spellman, in a public speech, mentioned disdainfully the "shibboleth" of separation. And only now, as far as I know, for the first time, the system of American separation of church and state has been rejected, nay denied to even exist, in an official statement of the American Catholic Church.

According to this statement, not separation but cooperation of church and state is the American legal tradition. The main evidence in support of this thesis is the words of the Northwest Ordinance of 1787, repeated in the Southwest Ordinance of 1790, which states: "Religion, morality and knowledge being necessary to good citizenship and the happiness of mankind, schools and the means of education shall forever be encouraged." This obviously means that schools in which religion, morality, and secular knowledge of all kinds is imparted shall be encouraged by the government. The temptation to read in these words more than there is in them and to take the vague general word "encourage" in the specific sense of financial aid by the state to religious denominational schools was too strong for the bishops, and so this interpretation plays a very important part in their statement on Christian action. But they would have resisted it if attention had been paid to the fact that all injunctions and laws, past and present of the legislative, and all the acts of the executive branches of the government of the United States, are all of them conditioned by the implicit and necessary clause "if permitted and within the limits permitted by the Constitution." The Ordinances of 1787 and 1790 are no exception: They must be interpreted in the light of the First Amendment.

There is no doubt that the founders of the American republic and the framers of its Constitution intended to create a Christian state in which institutions and laws should manifest a Christian spirit. But for most of them, or at least for such men as Thomas Jefferson and James Madison who played a prominent part in those events, this Christian spirit was not to be found so much in the dogmatic teaching or in the denominational institutions of churches and religious denominations as in the principles of equality and liberty, of brotherhood and respect of human personality which to them were the essential parts of the Christian message, and which they found also in the humanitarian trend of eighteenth-century philosophy. Even the most prominent Catholic layman of the times, the great champion of Catholic liberties, John Carroll of Carrollton, Maryland, had been somehow affected by those ideas during the years he spent in France, 1772–73, if it is true that, according to his biographer, he did not at all like to have around him priests and Jesuits.

But just because all of them believed that all men are created equal by God, they adopted the principle that all citizens should be equal before the law, with no discrimination as to faith or class, and no distinction between laymen and clergymen. Just because American democracy believed that religion, morality, and knowledge are necessary for good citizenship, the American laws have granted to all churches and religious organizations and institutions, to all schools, either religious or secular, to all cultural, social, and charitable nonprofit institutions, the great encouragement of exemption from taxation. But American democracy did not go further and cannot go further within the limits of the Constitution. The founders' idea of a Christian nation with such a liberal and broad reinterpretation of the Christian spirit was realized for the first time in the United States of America.

The Catholic attitude toward the American Constitution is affected by two opposite and irreconcilable forces. On the one hand, as Americans who have experienced the benefits of a regime of religious liberty, in comparison with the old system of union of church and state which meant practically the control of the church by the state, or vice versa, all Catholics express their thanks to God and their sincere feeling of gratitude and devotion to the Constitution. But on the other hand, the Catholic clergy, mindful of the papal rejection of Americanism, must acknowledge that the American system, though friendly to the Church, does not meet all the requirements and does not escape repudiation by the Church, because it does not admit the fundamental claim that Catholicism is the only true religion and all the implications of this claim.

To overcome this contrast of opposite forces, the American bishops have disclaimed solemnly in their statement "any intent or desire to alter the prudent and fair American policy of government in dealing with the delicate problems that have their source in the divided religious allegiance of our citizens." In making this solemn declaration, they speak as good Americans. But on the other hand, they propose an interpretation of the Constitution which would replace the principle of separation of church and state as practiced now by the principle of cooperation of church and state. Of course, it is their contention that they are not suggesting any change, because the "prudent and fair American policy" which they are eager to preserve is not that of separation but the supposed original policy of cooperation of church and state. What they advocate is a return to the original policy which now has been altered by secularism. We have seen how shaky are the premises on which this contention rests. But even if it were granted that it be sound, its adoption would change the actual system of relations of church and state. As Cardinal John Newman said, "Every reaction is always an innovation."

The Catholic bishops, in their wisdom and their knowledge of the internal conditions of their church, have found it advisable to raise now this question and to urge now upon American Catholics the organization of a kind of crusade to bring about this innovation. At this time, when most American minds under the threat, real or imaginary, of an onslaught from a savage totalitarianism of the left may be inclined to shift far enough toward the extreme right, such an innovation labeled as a restoration might have a chance of success. But it might also prove to be a boomerang. Though connected with religion, this is essentially a political question in which even bishops can make mistakes. Not a few Catholics may be inclined to disagree with them. To many non-Catholics who respect the Catholic Church, and to those who may have a certain sentimental attachment to Catholicism, this new move of the hierarchy will cause a revulsion of feeling. The hope expressed in the episcopal statement that some sections of American Protestantism may join the Catholic crusade may be nothing more than wishful thinking. It is more likely that this crusade, when it gets going, will have the effect of precipitating a strong coalition of all Protestant scattered forces. The present trend toward a fusion or a system of close interchurch union of Protestant denominations, which may be of great advantage to American religious life, is gaining ground slowly. If, however, this coalition is hastened under the stress and the urgent necessity of opposing a common front to the Catholic onslaught, it will inevitably assume a militant anti-Catholic character and will extend the conflict to all sections of American life.

Most Americans look upon the system of public schools as one of the greatest achievements, and the stronghold, of our democracy. Almost 50 percent of Catholic parents still send their children to the public schools, though the Church, reversing the policy sanctioned by the last Council of Baltimore, has for a long time made a mortal sin of such a practice. It is not conceivable that the large majority of non-Catholic Americans will assist passively and will offer no resistance to the introduction of innovations which would undermine the very existence of the whole public system of education.

The Catholic hierarchy in the United States up to recent times shunned all open political entanglements of the Church with the government. To be sure, often prominent members of the episcopate have acquired great influence upon local governments or even in Washington, playing the game discreetly behind a screen. Everybody knows something about the "powerhouses" in several great American cities. These, however, have been local or personal activities which did not engage the Church as such. But now, by trying to establish official economic ties between the American Catholic Church as a whole and the federal government, and in time with state and local governments, the Catholic hierarchy has departed from the policy of their predecessors and has openly taken a new direction.

It is not impossible that the coming crusade may succeed in bringing about a reversal of the decision of the Supreme Court in the *McCollum* case and then the grant by the federal government of financial support to Catholic schools. In terms of the financial burden now carried on by the Church, such a grant would be of great relief. But if the experience of the past is worth anything, if history teaches something, we cannot ignore the fact that the establishment of such ties, always and everywhere, sooner or later, has thrown the Church into the whirlpool of active politics. In order to protect such material gains from hostile political forces, the Church, sooner or later, has been forced to make alliances with all kinds of regimes, and political factions and parties, according to the changes in the political scenery. In most cases religions and churches have become instruments of political powers, *instrumentum regni*, subservient to the unholy interests of dominating forces. Politics is a hard game; it gives nothing for nothing. Certainly the American hierarchy of the Catholic Church has assumed a heavy responsibility. Its statement of November 1948 might, according to events, mark a turning point in American history.

PART TWO

AN AFTERWORD TO GEORGE LA PIANA

BY

JOHN M. SWOMLEY

5

THE VATICAN DOCTRINE AND STRATEGY FOR THE UNITED STATES

I have been asked to update the previous pages by George La Piana, the Roman Catholic priest-scholar noted for his distinguished academic work in Italy and in America, to which he immigrated in 1913. From 1916, when he taught at Harvard Divinity School, until his retirement in 1947 as the John H. Morison Professor of Church History, Professor La Piana was opposed to dictatorship and to bureaucratic demands evident in the Vatican and its control over the American hierarchy. He believed that it was essential to maintain American democracy free from papal control, though this obviously was possible only if Americans consciously were aware of the dangers of theocracy implicit in the Vatican's far-ranging influence.

Although my style of writing differs from his, I am faithfully pursuing his concern and conviction in an effort to contribute to his work to reform and democratize the

Roman Catholic Church in America. La Piana became a United States citizen in 1918 and was a firm opponent of the Vatican's support of fascism and totalitarianism during World War II. Indeed, he saw totalitarian parallels in the Vatican's attempt to operate in a democratic America.

The only place where I differ from Professor La Piana is in his understanding of the U.S. Constitution and separation of church and state, as evident in his concluding pages. He claims first that the Constitution forbids "the establishment of a religion" and hence an "official church" with "a religious monopoly and educational monopoly," and claims that "it was not the intention of the lawgivers to forbid . . . financial aid" to support churches and "church denominational schools." He supports this by referring to a controversy among Virginia delegates to Congress which he does not quote or document. His misunderstanding of the First Amendment is obvious when he wrote, "Congress shall make no law respecting the establishment of *a* religion," whereas it actually reads "respecting an establishment of religion."

Separation of religion and state was intended by Article VI, Section 3, which states that "no religious test shall ever be required as a qualification to any office or public trust under the United States." Some states refused to ratify the Constitution unless there was an amendment guaranteeing no support of religion. James Madison proposed an amendment that said, "nor shall any national religion be established . . ." but this was rejected. The final result of Senate and House debate was acceptance of the House statement, "Congress shall make no law respecting an establishment of religion." The word "respecting" means *concerning, touching upon,* or *with regard to.* Both Madison and Jefferson used the phrase "establishment of religion" as an institution of religion as well as establishment in terms of state support.

La Piana is mistaken also in assuming that Congress was "forbidding only an unequal treatment of religions," or "financial support to the established religion." There were six states that had multiple establishments in that they supported all churches in their states. It was this nonpreferential support that the Congress opposed and which all states subsequently rejected.

La Piana cites the Northwest Ordinance of 1787 as evidence of the American legal tradition of "not separation but cooperation of church and state." Actually the Continental Congress had considered in 1785 a Northwest Land Ordinance governing the settlement of territories west of the original colonies, in which one lot in every township was allowed for the maintenance of public schools and another lot proposed for the support of religion. However, the support for religion did not become part of that ordinance, nor was it in the continuance and expansion of the Ordinance of 1787. A complete discussion of the colonial practices concerning religion and the clear Constitutional context of separation of church is found in my book, *Religious Liberty and the Secular State.*

I am not a Roman Catholic, but I have learned much from Roman Catholic scholars such as Hans Küng, A. B. Hassler, Jon Sobrino, and other liberation theologians in Latin America; from Rosemary Radford Reuther and Joan Chitrister, among others, who have broadened my horizons and understanding of Roman Catholicism's worldwide reform movement. I have lectured at various Catholic organizations in Kansas and Missouri (including Conception Seminary) and at the large Roman Catholic seminary in Cordoba, Argentina; met with priests in Peru, Uruguay, and Argentina to discuss liberation theology and nonviolence; collaborated with the Marynoll missionary organization during the Sandinista government in Nicaragua; and served as African correspondent of the *National Catholic Reporter* in 1977. In 1994 I visited the small Catholic Church in Pyongyang, meeting with North Korean leaders in my capacity as executive of the American Committee on Korea in order to bolster that church's religious liberty. Earlier I organized Protestants and Roman Catholics in Argentina and the Philippines during the dictatorships there to work for freedom by nonviolent means.

My chief concern as a retired professor of Christian social ethics at the St. Paul School of Theology in Kansas City, Missouri, and as former chair of the Church-State Committee of the American Civil Liberties Union, is to maintain separation of church and state and to preserve it and religious liberty for all in the United States. Therefore, I work to oppose efforts by any religious group to impose its control over political, educational, and other institutions, including the media, the culture, and women and their reproductive freedom.

This afterword begins with the Second Vatican Council (1962–65) and its impact on the American branch of the Roman Catholic Church, as well as on the world Church. In one sense, the council changed public opinion greatly, yet it changed nothing in the Vatican's attempt to exercise authority over governmental policies.

The Second Vatican Council emphasized that the Roman Catholic Church was not simply the pope and the bishops but was also defined as "the people of God" who could use their own language in worship. It defined non-Roman churches as "separated brethren" rather than simply heretics and enemies, thus opening communication and cooperation between Roman Catholics and Protestants.

However, official Vatican control of the Church and official Roman Catholic doctrine did not change on any crucial points, so the purpose and program of the Vatican remained that of authoritarian control of Catholics and of governments. Religious liberty, democracy, and ecumenism were not authorized by the official documents of Vatican II. Both non-Catholics and Roman Catholics who have not read the documents have accepted erroneous assumptions that the Church had changed its position on these issues.

The traditional position of the Church, as formulated by Pope Leo XIII (1878–1903) and circulated in the United States in 1960 just before Vatican II, was that the state must not only have care for religion but must "recognize the true religion professed by the Catholic Church." It was a logical position if its premises were accepted. If the state is under moral compulsion to profess and promote religion, it is obliged to process and promote only the religion that is true; for no individual, no group of individuals, no society, no state is justified in supporting error or in according to error the same recognition as to truth.[1]

The Declaration of Religious Liberty that came out of

Vatican II affirms "traditional Catholic doctrines on the moral duty of men and societies toward the true religion and toward the one Church of Christ." It specifically says, "This one true religion subsists in the [Roman] Catholic and Apostolic Church." It also indicates that the declaration does not, in given circumstances, prevent particular religious groups from receiving "special civil recognition" from the state.

The Declaration of Religious Liberty speaks of the rights of parents "to determine . . . the kind of religious education that their children are to receive." This means that government "must acknowledge the right of parents to make a genuinely free choice of schools." According to the council's Declaration on Christian Education, free choice has nothing to do with parental options to send a child to a non-Church school, for "the Council also reminds Catholic parents of the duty of entrusting their children to Catholic schools." Rather, free choice means "that public subsidies are paid out in such a way that parents are truly free to choose." In this way, the Vatican Council has woven the idea of government aid to church schools (and therefore taxation of non-Catholics as well as Catholics) into its position on religious liberty.

The major new approach to religious liberty by Vatican II is the recognition that the religious liberty of non-Catholics is a "civil right," whereas for Catholics it is grounded in divine law and a "sacred freedom" which "is so much the property of the Church that to act against it is to act against the will of God." The "civil right" of non-Catholics to religious liberty is not set forth in the absolute terms reserved for the Roman Catholic Church but, rather, is grounded in present-day circumstances. In an October 2,

1965, editorial, the Jesuit weekly *America* acknowledged the shortcoming of the Declaration on Religious Liberty: "It is perhaps necessary to remind Americans that the Council is not about to enact the First Amendment of the United States Constitution as a Catholic doctrine."

Those who criticize the Roman Catholic Church's position on religious liberty generally make the point that it is difficult (if not impossible) for a church that denies liberty to its own laypeople, priests, and bishops to show much concern for the liberty of others outside the church. The Reverend Christopher C. Webber, an Episcopalian, has said that Catholic structural reform must begin within a system "in which no layman yet has a voice, no parish priest, bishop or cardinal is elected, in which no representative forms exist."[2]

In discussing such questions as attendance at religious ceremonies other than those of the Roman church or participation in weddings between non-Romans, he observes, "The basic theory is still that you must be guided in all such things by the hierarchy, that they will decide what is best for you and what you may do." Father Webber concludes by saying, "When all rules and power are placed in the hands of one man, however able and liberal and well advised, error is almost certain."

The official Vatican position on ecumenism also differs from the views of other Christian churches and is conditioned by the "one true church" theory. Many decades before the Vatican expressed an interest in ecumenism there was an ecumenical movement intended to foster cooperation and unity among Protestant and Orthodox churches. Agreements not to compete in mission fields abroad were one result of ecumenism. Another was the formation of federations of churches such as the Federal Council of Churches (which later became the National Council of Churches) and the World Council of Churches. Thus, one view of ecumenism is cooperative activity among equally valid churches organized in an ongoing federation or council.

The Vatican view of ecumenism is that all Christians should be unified in one Christian body. During the Second Vatican Council, Pope Paul VI announced that such unity cannot be attained except by identity of faith, by participation in the same sacraments, and in the organic harmony of a single ecclesiastical control. He also asserted that only the Catholic Church can offer these elements. This is also the position of the Second Vatican's decree on ecumenism.

A second view of ecumenism was advanced during Vatican II in *Lumen Gentium*, which said, "This church of Christ is truly present in all legitimate local congregations of the faithful which, united with their pastors, are called Churches in the New Testament." However, Brazilian theologian Leonardo Boff was silenced when he advanced the interpretation that all first-century churches, and hence modern churches, are as valid as the Roman Church.

The continuing emphasis on the Roman Church as the "one true church" is crucial to its attempt to change certain major United States government policies. In its effort to establish such policy-making authority, the Vatican or the U.S. hierarchy has adopted at least five strategies. These strategies, which are not discussed in chronological order, include one which effectively silences American Protestants.

The Catholic hierarchy has arranged unilateral dialogues

with each of various Protestant churches, such as the Episcopalians, Methodists, and Lutherans, with no publicity given to the ongoing dialogues. In fact, the Roman hierarchy has imposed a rule that dialogue partners must not engage in public criticism of each other. This effectively means that Protestant churches, their journals, and hence their theologians, are precluded from critical analysis of the Roman church on a variety of issues. This further means that the Vatican and its agents are free to function politically to influence government decisions without public criticism by Protestant bodies about the exercise of Catholic power. The chief criticisms of the efforts of a totalitarian church to dominate cultures and governments have come from progressive Roman Catholics, who criticize such domination (known as "triumphalism") and then are silenced.

The second Vatican strategy is to silence important Catholic critics who deviate from the official Vatican position. The world's leading Catholic theologian, Hans Küng, referred to this in a long statement published in the October 11, 1985, *National Catholic Reporter*: "No one is burned at the stake anymore, but careers and psyches are destroyed as required." Priests and theologians are "dismissed and suspended from ecclesiastical functions." This is enforced by Cardinal Joseph Ratzinger, who heads what used to be called the "Holy Office of the Roman and Universal Inquisition" and for public relations purposes has been renamed the "Congregation for the Doctrine of the Faith."

The effort to dominate governments begins with the silencing of any critical movement within the church or state, such as liberation theology or communities of the poor in Latin America. Küng wrote, "In very important cases, such as the recalcitrant Latin American episcopate, Ratzinger journeys with a whole posse to the relevant country to make unequivocally clear what the 'Catholic truth' is. Alternatively (as in the case of Holland and Switzerland) a whole episcopate is invited to Rome for a 'closed session'—as the new instrument of curial domination."[3]

In the United States, the Vatican has followed a similar pattern. The leading Catholic journalist, Penny Lernoux, described in her book, *The People of God,* the origin of the Vatican campaign to eliminate Catholic deviance from papal control. In her chapter, "The Roman Restoration in the United States," Lernoux noted that "the church was not Vatican II's 'People of God' but those who did not engage in dissent." It was a "grave error", said the pope, to believe that those who selectively dissented from church teachings (e.g., on birth control) could still be "good Catholics."[4]

Lernoux wrote that "[Pope] John Paul was determined to discipline the American church. Signs of the coming storm were evident in the early 1980s when Rome attempted to discipline American nuns, but what brought home the conflict was the punishment of Seattle's Archbishop Raymond Hunthausen, who was stripped of his powers in 1986."[5] He was made an example to the other bishops partly because he did not come from an influential or financially important diocese. Lernoux described the Vatican's investigation of Hunthausen in 1983 as follows:

> In the peculiarly medieval fashion whereby the
> Vatican undertakes such inquiries, the accused is

not allowed to know the charges, has no access to the proceedings, and is not shown the results. Essentially the accused is permitted no means of defense. Thus for two years Hunthausen was kept in the dark about interviews conducted in his own archdiocese. Documents were sent to Rome without his knowledge, and he was not permitted to see the final report.[6]

The pope's agent who handled the inquisition was Archbishop Pio Laghi, who was earlier the papal representative in Argentina who worked with the military in their atrocities against suspected dissidents known as the "disappeared." Emilio Mignone, an Argentine Catholic and author of *Witness to the Truth: The Complicity of Church and Dictatorship in Argentina,* reported Laghi's "papal blessing" to the commanders and officers in the army who were involved in "anti-subversive operations." Mignone wrote, "The military took on part of the responsibility for the task of cleaning the dirty courtyard of the church, with the acquiescence of the bishops" who stood by "watching unmoved as bishops, priests, religious and ordinary Christians are murdered, abducted, tortured, jailed, exiled and slandered."[7]

In the United States, the bishops and cardinals similarly refrained from openly supporting Hunthausen. They were aware that the pope had disciplined Hunthausen for his peace position during the Cold War against the Soviets, his support of greater participation by women in the church, and his modest departure from papal teaching on sexual norms, among others.

Another papal action was begun in 1979 against the Rev.

Charles Curran, who had taught moral theology for twenty years at the Catholic University of America. He was officially informed by Cardinal Ratzinger in Rome that he was "no longer . . . suitable or eligible" to teach Catholic theology at the university. Charles Curran's case received wide publicity and was, therefore, another assertion of Vatican power that could not be ignored by Catholic educational institutions in the United States.

About the same time, the Congregation for Catholic Education in Rome, headed by Cardinal William Baum, an American with subservience to authority but no experience in education, set forth a schema that proposed that local bishops could assert control of any teacher in Catholic colleges who lacked "doctrinal integrity and uprightness of life" by dismissing him. He could also "declare the university to be no longer Catholic."

The net effect of the Curran dismissal, as well as the schema, was to stop criticism by university professors of Vatican positions or actions. The Vatican also moved against American nuns, forcing them to resign from public office or from their religious order. The only group that did not completely buckle under pressure was the Coalition of American Nuns, even though they were told that it was "inappropriate" for women's religious orders to take positions against U.S. policies, for example, in Central America. Nevertheless, with few exceptions, the Vatican has succeeded in forcing the administrative and intellectual leadership of the American Church to become thoroughgoing agents of papal totalitarianism.

We turn now to the papal attempt to control minds and votes of Catholic lay politicians and voters. This third aspect

of Vatican strategy is to use influential Catholic laity to function politically without apparent connection to the Vatican
or the hierarchy. A major study of the Vatican's use of
Catholic laity throughout Europe was made by Catholic
professor Jean-Guy Villaincourt of the University of Mon-
treal in his book *Papal Power: A Study of Vatican Control over
Lay Catholic Elites.* Villaincourt in his concluding summary
said in part, "The Catholic lay militant has been pressed into
service as an . . . intermediary between the Papacy and the
modern state."[8] In Europe, it is Catholic Action and the
Christian Democratic party which assume "direct political
responsibilities" that the hierarchy must shun.

In the United States, there have for decades been selected
right wing Catholic laity who promote Vatican issues.
Among those sometimes regarded as such loyalists are
William Buckley, Hugh Carey, William B. Casey, Wiliam B.
Ball, Joseph Grace, William Simon, and Henry Hyde. For
many years there have been such organizations as the
Knights of Columbus and the Knights of Malta, whose mis-
sion has also been the promotion of a Vatican agenda.

In 1991 an important new organization known as the
Catholic Campaign for America (CCA) was organized to
promote essentially the right-wing program of Pope John
Paul II. Its "ecclesiastical advisor" was Cardinal John
O'Connor, but the laity on the CCA board and national
committee function without publicizing their role in the
organization. Among them are William J. Bennett, who was
Pres. Ronald Reagan's secretary of education and who often
appeared with Sen. Bob Dole as his advisor on vouchers for
parochial schools, and presidential candidate Patrick

Buchanan, whose role was to maintain a hard-line stance on the Catholic agenda so that the Republican platform would reflect this position. Buchanan insisted on continuing in the 1996 primaries even after it was obvious he could not win the nomination. He said he was "not after any seat or promotion or anything like that" but wanted "to remake and reshape the Republican Party."[9] He insisted that his major aim was to keep the "right-to-life" plank in the Republican platform.

The overall mission of the Catholic Campaign for America is "to activate Catholic citizens, increase the Catholic electorate's influence in formulating public policy, and focus the public's attention on the richness and beauty of Catholic teaching."[10] A 1992 newsletter of the Catholic Campaign declared that "separation of church and state is a false premise that must finally be cast aside."[11]

In practice the leaders of the CCA are almost entirely key Republicans. In addition to those already mentioned are 1996 presidential candidate Robert K. Dornan; Richard Santorum, member of the Senate from Pennsylvania; several former ambassadors to the Vatican; Judge James L. Ryan, U.S. Court of Appeals, Sixth District; and Phyllis Schlafly.

In addition to the CCA, there are major Catholic-led right-wing lay organizations established in Washington which promote the Vatican agenda. These include the Heritage Foundation set up by Paul Weyrich and another Weyrich-founded group, the Free Congress Research and Education Foundation, which also operates National Empowerment Television, whose chairman is William J. Bennett. These organizations function without any reference either to Catholic or other far-right agendas, and are frequently described in the press simply as conservative organizations or as think tanks.

The fourth major strategy of the Vatican to dominate government is to use abortion and birth control as issues with which to build a Catholic-led political ecumenical movement whose purpose is to write papal doctrine on these issues into U.S. law.

On November 20, 1975, the U.S. Catholic bishops issued their Pastoral Plan for Pro-Life Activities, which is a detailed blueprint for controlling the American democratic process at local, state, and national levels. It did so by creating a political machine controlled at each level by the bishops. Timothy Byrnes in his book *Catholic Bishops in American Politics* called it "the most focused and aggressive political leadership" ever planned and executed by the U.S. Catholic hierarchy.[12] The Bishops' plan states, "It is absolutely necessary to encourage the development in each congressional district of an identifiable, tightly knit and well-organized pro-life unit. This unit can be described as a public interest group or a citizens' lobby."[13] The plan of action then lists twenty Catholic organizations to mobilize the Church. These include priests and religious orders, the Knights of Columbus, Catholic Lawyers Association, Catholic Physicians Guild, Catholic Press Association, and Catholic nurses and social workers groups, among others. It even includes the government-assisted National Conference of Catholic Charities. All are expected to function against abortion and birth control in each congressional district.

The Bishops' plan calls for the "appointment of judges" who will "reverse Roe and Doe [*Roe* v. *Wade* and *Doe* v. *Bolton*, the Supreme Court's 1973 abortion rights rulings] and for law professors and lawyers to write articles for law journals attacking the philosophical basis of Roe and Doe."[14] It calls for each diocese to establish a pro-life committee and for a continuing effort to go after each senator and congressman. One of the early successes of the Bishops' plan was the passage of the Hyde Amendment, which restricted the use of Medicaid money for abortions, limiting poor women's access to abortion. Although declared unconstitutional by a federal district court judge, an appeals court overturned that decision and it became law.

The Bishops' plan also indicates that their action against abortion must not be thought of as a Catholic movement, but must be seen as ecumenical. This was probably their most important decision because it resulted in the enlistment of much of the Protestant right-wing as both allies and followers of the bishops' strategy. The bishops, using the strategy described earlier of working through Catholic laity, were successful in getting certain fundamentalist right-wing groups to adopt their agenda.

One of the early Catholic leaders was conservative writer William F. Buckley, Jr., who founded Young Americans for Freedom at his Sharon, Connecticut, estate in 1960. He was also very influential in the 1964 organization of the American Conservative Union, which was the forerunner of a number of existing rightist groups, such as the Conservative Caucus and the National Conservative Political Action Committee. Probably the most influential of all the early Catholic leaders, however, is Paul Weyrich, whose Free Congress Foundation lent support to the "lengthy campaign" which led to the Vatican's disciplining of Archbishop Hunthausen. It was Weyrich, together with Ed McAteer and Howard Phillips, who spent a day with Jerry Falwell persuading him to take on the issue of abortion. Ed McAteer is cofounder of the Religious Round-table; Howard Phillips is founder of the Conservative Caucus. As Connie Paige notes in her book *The Right-to-Lifers*, out of that meeting also "came the idea for the Moral Majority, the single most crucial entity since the Catholic Church in making the right-to-life movement a dangerous force on the right."[15]

"At that meeting in Lynchburg, Virginia, in January 1979," Paige continues, "Paul Weyrich was the one who articulated exactly what it was they all were trying to accomplish."[16] Richard Viguerie, in his book *The New Right*, put it this way: "Paul Weyrich and Howard Phillips spent countless hours with electronic ministers like Jerry Falwell, James Robison, and Pat Robertson, urging them to get involved in conservative politics."[17]

It seems clear that Jerry Falwell's Moral Majority and Pat Robertson's Christian Coalition would not have been organized if the Vatican through its agents, the American bishops, had not decided it was necessary to involve articulate right-wing Protestant leaders in their antiabortion campaign. When the Moral Majority was organized, it was not simply a Protestant evangelical group. "Jerry Falwell estimated that nearly one-third of the Moral Majority's members were Roman Catholic."[18] The Christian Coalition, according to its executive, Ralph Reed, "revealed a similarly strong presence of Catholic supporters."[19]

Richard Viguerie was himself a Roman Catholic political activist, influential in recruiting right-wing Protestants. Early in his career he started his own direct-mail company and in 1973 he began working for racist Governor George Wallace of Alabama. While doing his work for Wallace, Viguerie picked up mailing lists of Wallace's segregationist and fundamentalist following. By 1981 the Viguerie Company had 250 employees; in addition to fund-raising, he was publishing the *Conservative Digest* and the *New Right Report.* Viguerie also raised money for Jesse Helms's reelection to the Senate and accumulated more names and addresses of contributors to his list.

Another pair of right-wing Catholics, Paul and Judie Brown, were the ones who actually organized fundamentalist Protestants into their own version of the right-to-life movement. In addition to inviting them to meetings, the Browns offered to do the fundamentalists' mailings—in the process getting a percentage of the money raised through direct-mail fund-raising, keeping an eye on what was being sent, and acquiring a whole new list of names for their own use. As Connie Paige reported in *The New Right-to-Lifers,* the Browns also teamed up with key Mormon leaders to bring them into right-to-life activities.

This list of right-wing Catholics coopting Protestant fundamentalists is far from complete. However, it does reveal how clearly the Catholic right has led the Protestant fundamentalists. According to the report, *A New Rite: Conservative Catholic Organizations and Their Allies,* prepared by Catholics for a Free Choice, "Many national committee members of the Catholic Campaign for America are long-time associates of Pat Robertson. In addition, the Catholic organizations in this directory often cooperate with groups such as the Family Research Council, the Christian Coalition, Operation Rescue, Focus on the Family, and the Traditional Values Coalition."[20] Key figures in the Catholic hierarchy, such as Cardinal John O'Connor, have cooperated in this endeavor. O'Connor, for example, introduced Pat Robertson to the pope during the pope's 1995 visit to New York City. According to *A New Rite*, "More than 100,000 voter guides produced by Pat Robertson were distributed in Catholic parishes throughout New York City" in 1993 "to influence school board elections."[21]

Other developments reveal the success of the bishops' strategy. The Southern Baptist Convention came under right-wing control and accepted the Catholic position on abortion. And on March 29, 1995, Cardinal O'Connor; Pat Robertson; Catholic Bishop Francis George of Yakima, Washington; Archbishop Francis Stafford of Denver; Bishop Carlos A. Sevilla of San Francisco; Harvard Professor Mary Ann Glendon; Father Richard John Neuhaus; convicted Watergate conspirator Charles Colson; and others signed and endorsed "Evangelicals and Catholics Together: The Christian Mission in the Third Millennium." And on December 9, 1995, the Christian Coalition launched the Catholic Alliance, which Ralph Reed described as "a fully owned subsidiary" or "auxiliary" of the Christian Coalition. The Catholic Alliance was announced in a massive mailing to Roman Catholics which carried this message from Ralph Reed: "[The] Christian Coalition launched the Catholic Alliance in 1995 because Catholics already make up 16.3 [percent] of Christian Coalition's 1.6 million members, and we need to expand Christian Coalition's Catholic representation."[22] By coopting Southern Baptists and other fundamentalist groups, the bishops are able to pick up significant numbers of votes in Congress for papal positions.

The fifth strategy of the American hierarchy involves the direct intervention of the Vatican and the bishops themselves. The evidence for this is overwhelming. For example, on June 25, 1992, the Vatican released a statement to all U.S. bishops which began, "Recently legislation has been proposed in some American states which would make discrimination on the basis of sexual orientation illegal."[23] The Vatican then provided a list of categories where it believed discrimination should be legal, including teachers, coaches, tenants, adoption and foster care personnel, and it recommended prohibiting the extension of company health benefits to an employee's homosexual partner.

Then Pope John Paul II explicitly intervened in the American political process on March 26, 1995, with a papal encyclical, *Evangelium Vitae*, requiring the obedience of Roman Catholic voters, legislators, and judges. The following are crucial sentences in a much longer papal decree:

> No circumstances, no purpose, no law whatsoever can ever make licit an act which is intrinsically illicit, since it is contrary to the Law of God which is written in every heart, knowable by reason itself, and proclaimed by the church.
>
> Abortion and euthanasia are thus crimes which no human law can claim to legitimize. There is no obligation in conscience to obey such laws; instead there is grave and clear obligation to oppose them by conscientious objection.
>
> In the case of an intrinsically unjust law, such as a law permitting abortion or euthanasia, it is never

licit to obey it, or to take part in a propaganda campaign in favor of such a law, or vote for it.

The pope also insisted that his authority to interpret what is moral must be placed ahead of democratic judgments of people whose interpretation of the will of God differs from his. He specifically stated, "Democracy cannot be idolized to the point of making it a substitute for morality." He also said, "As a result we have what appear to be dramatically opposed tendencies."[24]

In the 1996 presidential election, candidate Robert Dole made a major speech to the Catholic Press Association's annual convention in Philadelphia on May 3, in which he endorsed "school choice," which involves the funding of parochial schools through tuition vouchers. He also attacked President Bill Clinton's late-term abortion veto and, in the context of abortion, said, "Though not a Catholic, I would listen to Pope John Paul II."[25] Immediately following that speech, Dole had a twenty-minute meeting with Cardinal Anthony Bevilacqua of Philadelphia. On June 25, Dole had an hour-long private meeting with Cardinal John O'Connor of New York City in which they discussed Dole's commitment to the papal position on abortion.

When a reporter asked O'Connor if he was comfortable with Dole's reported effort to seek tolerance for pro-choice Republicans, the cardinal endorsed Dole's plan saying, "I cannot imagine that Senator Dole will deviate from his commitment on abortion." He also said, "I think that Senator Dole has a wonderfully pro-life record and I doubt very much that's going to change in any significant way."[26]

Although Dole did not request a joint photo, the cardinal posed with Dole for a picture for the *New York Times* which appeared the next day on the front page as an obvious endorsement.

On July 18, Dole spoke to a Catholic audience at Cardinal Stritch College in Milwaukee where, according to the *New York Times,* he emphasized his proposal for "vouchers paying $1,000 a year in tuition for pupils in grades one through eight and $1,500 a year for high school students. States that had adopted voucher programs would apply for federal assistance," and the "federal government would provide $2.5 billion a year to be matched" by the state.[27]

Bob Dole chose Rep. Henry Hyde, who is generally regarded as the Catholic bishops' spokesperson in Congress, as head of the Republican platform committee. Hyde, in turn, according to the *National Catholic Reporter,* invited Catholics to help him develop the party's 1996 platform. In an open letter to Catholics, Hyde wrote, "Catholics are a powerful voice for moral authority and fulfill a growing leadership role in the Republican Party," noting that "there are nine U.S. senators, fifty-five members of the House, and nine governors who are both Republican and Catholic." His letter also said, "As a Catholic, I believe the basic principles of Catholic teaching are philosophically and morally aligned with those of the Republican Party."[28]

It is even more significant that the Catholic bishops took action to aid the Republican Party. The president of the National Conference of Catholic Bishops, Anthony M. Pilla of Cleveland, departed from custom to tell the 250 bishops that, although they should not engage in partisan politics, they could address political issues that might be closer to the views of one party. Then, after a "stinging attack on President Clinton's veto of a measure that banned a type of late term abortion," the bishops, according to the *New York Times,* "unanimously endorsed [Dole's] appeal to Congress to overturn the veto."[29] The *New York Times* reported that orders had been placed by the Conference of Bishops for more than 9 million sets of postcards to be sent by constituents to their Representatives urging Congress to overturn the veto. This political campaign obviously made the bishops' political position felt throughout the country. On no issue other than abortion and birth control have the bishops been so openly active. The reason has been clearly stated by the Vatican point man in the United States, Cardinal John O'Connor. In an April 3, 1992, speech to the most right-wing of Catholic universities, Franciscan University of Steubenville, Ohio, he said, "The fact is that attacks on the Catholic church's stance on abortion, unless they are rebutted effectively, erode church authority in all matters, indeed the authority of God himself."[30] He said, according to the April 9, 1992, edition of his newspaper, *Catholic New York,* "Abortion has become the number one challenge for the Church in the United States because . . . if the Church's authority is rejected on such a crucial question as human life . . . then questioning of the Trinity becomes child's play, as does the divinity of Christ or any other Church teaching."

The Catholic bishops have decided to try to impose papal authority in the United States through the abortion issue. Their Committee for Pro-Life Activities is the best funded of the bishops' thirteen secretariats and committees, with a budget of $1.8 million in 1993. According to the latest published information by Catholics for a Free Choice,[31] the committee's budget is more than three times the next largest budget, that of the Secretariat for Ecumenical and InterReligious Affairs, and four times the budget of the Secretariat for Laity, Women, Family, and Youth.

The abortion issue is also a cover for opposition to birth control, since the Vatican claims that contraceptives which function after intercourse—such as the "morning after" pill or an intrauterine device—are really abortifacients because they operate to prevent implantation of the fertilized egg in the uterus. Therefore, all family planning programs worldwide, other than natural family planning, are opposed.

The bishops were successful in dominating the Reagan and Bush administrations on this issue, as revealed in the February 4, 1992, issue of *Time* magazine. That article, entitled "The U.S. and the Vatican on Birth Control," began with this sentence: "In response to concerns of the Vatican, the Reagan Administration agreed to alter its foreign aid program to comply with the church's teaching on birth control." According to William Wilson, the first U.S. ambassador to the Holy See after Reagan established diplomatic recognition, this resulted in the withdrawal of U.S. funding of international family planning organizations, including the United Nations Fund for Population Activities.

"American policy was changed as a result of the Vatican's not agreeing with our policy," Wilson asserted. "American aid programs around the world did not meet the criteria the Vatican administration had for family planning." Therefore, when the Reagan administration sent State Department representatives to Rome, Wilson said, "I'd accompany them to meet the president of the Pontifical Council for the Family."

In an accompanying article in the same issue of *Time*, there is a report of Reagan's first meeting with the pope in 1982 and of other meetings between the Vatican's U.S. representative, Pio Laghi, and Reagan officials. According to that article, the key administration players were all devout Roman Catholics: CIA director William Casey, National Security Advisor Richard Allen, National Security Advisor William Clark, Secretary of State Alexander Haig, Ambassador-at-Large Vernon Walters, as well as Wilson.

Reagan's collaboration with the Vatican seriously impeded family planning activities in many countries, including curtailing the availability of contraceptives, and thereby contributed to increasing the total world population. The United Nations Fund for Population Activities in 1991 stated, "World population, which reached 5.4 billion in mid-1991, is growing faster than ever before: three people every second, more than 250,000 every day. At the beginning of the decade the annual addition was 93 million."[32]

The consequences are enormous. The editor of the *National Catholic Reporter*, in an editorial in the June 19, 1992, issue, said, "I feel the church is causing great harm to the planet, making millions suffer unnecessarily. . . . Among today's 5.2 billion as many as one-fifth, mostly children, are undernourished. About 1 million die from hunger or hunger-related causes yearly" (estimates vary, however). The 1992 UNICEF report "State of the World's Children" said that a quarter of a million are allowed to die every week from malnutrition-related causes; that is 13 million a year. Moreover, those hunger-related problems have led to massive economic migrations which, in turn, have led to population wars such as those in Somalia, Rwanda, and Burundi according to *World Watch* magazine.[33] There are now, according to the *1996 World Almanac,* 5.8 million refugees in Africa and nearly 5.5 million in the Middle East, to say nothing of the economic migration into California, Texas, and Florida from Mexico, Central and South America, Haiti, and Cuba.

In short, the Reagan-Bush-Dole policy of collaborating with the Vatican has had serious effects on U.S. foreign and domestic policy.

Nevertheless, it is important to note that the hierarchy and the Republican candidates misjudged the Catholic vote, which is far more progressive than the Vatican's. All twelve of the most predominantly Catholic states went for the Democrats in the 1996 presidential election. This does not, however, minimize the Vatican threat to American democracy or its clear intent to establish its policies in the United States.

The Catholic hierarchy has every right to seek through political action to achieve its legislative goals, even when instructed by the pope to do so. It is also clear that those who oppose a foreign dictator's effort to impose his will on America have every right to analyze and oppose his efforts to achieve his goals.

6

CENSORSHIP
AND INTIMIDATION
OF THE PRESS

One of the ways in which the Vatican exercises its
totalitarianism in the United States is through censorship of the press so as to control public opinion. The
Knights of Columbus, for example, has for many years tried
to shut down any criticism of the Catholic church. In 1914
it created a Commission on Religious Prejudice and began a
campaign "of informing and correcting editors and journalists" who published items critical of the Catholic church.[1] As
a result of this pressure, few newspapers reported on the
political activities of that church.

In a rare report, New York's *Newsday,* in October 1993,
revealed that at least 83 percent of the income of the Archdiocese of New York comes from local, state, and federal taxes.[2]

For many years the Catholic church in the United States has
pressured newspapers and advertisers through boycotts and
other measures against the press, so that George Seldes, one of

America's great independent journalists, wrote in November 1981 that all of America's 1,750 daily papers were similarly terrified by "the Catholic Church's propaganda campaign."[3]

Since 1973 the spearhead of the Vatican's campaign to control the press and media has been the Catholic League for Religious and Civil Rights, founded by Jesuit priest Virgil Blum, who in 1959 organized Citizens for Educational Freedom to launch the campaign for vouchers by which government would give aid to parochial schools using parents as a conduit.

The purpose of the Catholic League is to suppress information that is critical of the Catholic church or puts it in a bad light. It does so by a variety of methods involving demands for an apology and retraction made to the reporter, editor, and publisher, by threats to the business office, and by boycotts of advertisers, among others. The Catholic League is not simply a collection of individuals. It exists in response to Canon 1369 of the Code of Canon Law: "A person is to be punished with a just penalty, who, at a public event or assembly, or in a published writing, or by otherwise using the means of social communication, utters blasphemy, or gravely harms public morals, or rails at or excites hatred or contempt for religion or the Church."[4]

William Donohue, who has led the Catholic League since 1993, claims that the league has "the support of all the U.S. cardinals and many of the bishops as well."[5] In other words, this seemingly unofficial group of mostly laypersons is implementing official church policy.

Donohue has on various occasions stated the league's strategy: "We specialize in public embarrassment of public figures who have earned our wrath, and that is why we are able to win so many battles: no person or organization wants to be publicly embarrassed, and that is why we specialize in doing exactly that."[6] He also wrote, "The threat of lawsuit is the only language that some people understand. The specter of public humiliation is another weapon that must be used. Petitions and boycotts are helpful. The use of the bully pulpit—via the airwaves—is a most effective strategy. Press conferences can be used to enlighten or alternatively to embarrass."[7]

Before Pope John Paul II visited the United States in October 1995, the Catholic League launched a campaign to intimidate the press and media so as to avoid reporting of any criticism of the pope. The league collected thousands of signatures from its members for the following petition:

> We, the undersigned, call on the media to act responsibly when Pope John Paul II comes to New York in October. It is not acting responsibly to give a high profile to the voices of dissident and alienated Catholics. It is not acting responsibly to focus almost exclusively on those issues of Catholic teaching that are in tension with the values of the culture; worse, it is wrong to lecture the Church on getting into line. It is not acting responsibly to neglect coverage of the good work that Catholics and the Catholic Church have done in servicing the least among us. It is not acting responsibly to deny that anti-Catholic sentiment is a force in our society. . . . [8]

It is worth noting that the above petition objects to reporting protests by Catholic dissidents and believes that "Catholic tensions" with American culture should be offset by the good work done by those Catholics who themselves are restricted or dominated by the Vatican.

The league's campaign largely succeeded in intimidating the press. The November 1995 issue of the *Catalyst,* its journal, carried the headline, "Media Treat Pope Fairly; Protesters Fail to Score." Donohue wrote, "From beginning to end, this papal visit proved to be the most triumphant of them all. . . . The relatively few cheap shots that were taken at the Pope by the media in October is testimony to a change in the culture." In other words, the "change in the culture" is the elevation of the pope and hierarchy to a position above criticism.

The Catholic League claims that any criticism of the pope, the hierarchy, and the Vatican is bigotry. The league, for example, has attacked CBS's *60 Minutes* for a January 22, 1995, broadcast featuring the progressive Catholic group, Call to Action.[9] It attacked *NBC Nightly News* for referring to Catholics for a Free Choice and another Catholic group, Dignity.[10] When the Associated Press mentioned that a federal appeals court judge who barred doctors from engaging in assisted suicide is a Catholic, the league launched a protest against AP that resulted in an AP apology. Donohue notes that "It will not have to call attention to such errors in the future."[11] In other words, the league's threat to the American press is clear—it is not permissible to identify public servants as Catholics when their public actions uphold papal teachings.

The Catholic League has called upon a Los Angeles radio

station, KFI, to fire its talk show host Bill Press, a Roman
Catholic, for remarks critical of the pope. [12] It has criticized
Fox TV, the cable network *Bravo*, advice columnist Ann Lan-
ders, ABC, *Newsday*, and numerous other media organiza-
tions for critical comments about the pope or the Catholic
Church. One result was a decision by the *Milwaukee Journal
Sentinel* to drop Ann Landers's column.[13]

The league has also attacked colleges for remarks professors
made in the classroom, or for cartoons run in a student newspaper at the University of Michigan. After a threatening letter
by Donahue to the president of the university, the cartoonist
apologized and the president wrote a conciliatory letter.[14]

The league has threatened members of Congress, both
House and Senate, calling on them to resign from the Population Institute because the institute's May 1995 fund-
raising letter contained the following sentence: "The Vatican
continues to undermine the advancements we've made in
Cairo [at the 1994 International Conference on Population
and Development] on issues of pregnancy prevention. The
anti-contraceptive gestapo has vowed to double the number
of its delegation to 28 and to turn once more to weaken the
cause of reproductive rights."[15]

In October 1994, the *Catalyst* carried this headline:
"League Assails Clinton Administration for Bigotry"
because of a State Department spokesperson's disagreement
with the Vatican over the Cairo Conference on population;
and the league published an "Open Letter" to the president
in the *New York Times* as an advertisement, asking President
Clinton to apologize for the State Department
spokesperson's statement.

The Catholic League has attacked government employees and even the Anti-Defamation League, a Jewish organization, for its decision to present a literary award to Richard Lukas for his book *Did the Children Cry? Hitler's War against Jewish and Polish Children.* In short, the Catholic League has increasingly been an agent for censorship of any critique of the Catholic Church and for the establishment of a Catholic culture as the norm in American public relations.[16]

In the fall of 1997 ABC launched a series called *Nothing Sacred* about a modern day priest who occasionally has doubts about his calling and in an opening segment tells a woman who confesses her intention to have an abortion that she should follow her own conscience. Catholic League objections brought about the cancellation of sponsorship by fifteen national sponsors such as Isuzu, Weight Watchers, Chrysler-Plymouth, and American Honda.[17]

In a directory of right-wing Catholic organizations published by Catholics for a Free Choice, the Catholic League's main office is listed as 1011 First Ave., New York, N.Y., which is the headquarters of the New York cardinal's archdiocese.

Democracy depends on the free flow of information and opinion and the people's right to know. There is a serious danger to any society or government when the leaders of any church or secret organization under their control can intimidate the press and media to suppress information and opinion. The people need to know when taxes are used to finance church institutions or when churches use political and judicial power to write church doctrines into law. Ultimately church, state, and the media face a decline in public confidence when important information is suppressed.

7

THE IMPACT OF
PAPAL INFALLIBILITY

The power of the pope and the Vatican has been rooted in the idea that the Roman Catholic Church is the one true church and that the Bishop of Rome speaks as the vicar or representative of Christ. These ideas, however, were not enough to maintain papal influence in Europe when the papacy lost its secular power because of the secularization set in motion by the French Revolution and the loss of the Papal States.

Once the process began, the Church no longer was able to arrest and execute people it considered revolutionaries or heretics. Moreover, it was losing influence and power as a result of the intellectual, industrial, and democratic revolutions. So at the First Vatican Council on July 18, 1870, two dogmas were proclaimed. One was the primacy of papal or universal jurisdiction, which, according to Hans Küng, reduced the various bishops to mere lackeys of Rome. The second was the dogma of papal infallibility, which means that the pope is incapable of error when he makes decisions *"ex cathedra"* on matters of faith and morals. However, the scope of papal infallibility has been stretched to include virtually all social and political decisions, depending on how they are framed. In any event, the pope's decisions are final.

Küng noted that "Infallibility performed the function of a metadogma, shielding and insuring all the other dogmas (and the innumerable doctrines and practices bound up in them). With infallibility—and the infallible aura of the 'ordinary' day-to-day magisterium is often more important than the relatively rare infallible definitions—the faithful seemed to have been given a superhuman protection and security which made them forget all fear of human uncertainty."[1]

The first casualty of "infallibility" is freedom within the church to disagree or dissent with respect to papal teaching or pronouncements. The only recourse of those who dissent is silence or disobedience. Disobedience has led to punishment of dissenters in various countries, including officially silencing them or forbidding them to teach in Catholic universities or even excommunication. These verdicts are handed out by what used to be called the Holy Office of the Roman and Universal Inquisition, now called the Congregation for the Doctrine of the Faith. Hans Küng, who was forbidden to teach in a Catholic university, wrote, "No one is burned at the stake anymore, but careers and psyches are destroyed as required."[2]

Since the doctrine of papal infallibility was intended to solidify papal power and prevent its erosion by dissent, the failure to stifle dissent required new and harsher methods. Therefore, according to a March 17, 1989, report in the

National Catholic Reporter, a new fidelity or loyalty oath must be "taken with both hands on a Bible, requiring teachers in any universities whatsoever who teaches disciplines which deal with faith or morals" as well as pastors, deacons, seminary rectors, and rectors of universities to do so. It is binding also on diocesan officials.

The oath requires obedience to whatever may issue in the future from the Vatican or bishops as well as what has already been proclaimed. One of the sentences in the oath says, "With Christian obedience I shall associate myself with what is expressed by the holy shepherds as authentic doctors and teachers of the faith or established by them as the Church's rulers."

The doctrine of infallibility has consequently become a totalitarian obedience to or thought control by the monarch. When the pope decides that a position he takes on morals, such as opposition to birth control or abortion, must not only be obeyed by the Catholic faithful, but must be legislated by the state, as he has done in the United States, he goes beyond control over citizens who do not accept his leadership or subscribe to his religious doctrine. Therefore the second casualty of infallibility is that church doctrine becomes political ideology. That in turn tends to alienate non-Catholics as well as Catholics who believe the mission of the Church is persuasive, nonpartisan, and service-oriented.

The third casualty of infallibility is recognition of the fact that no one, whatever his or her position of authority, is immune from error.

Among the many mistakes made by the papacy are those listed by Hans Küng, as follows: "the excommunication of

Photius, the Ecumenical Patriarch of Constantinople and of the Greek Church, which made formal the schism with the Eastern Church, a schism which is now almost a thousand years old; the prohibition of charging interest at the beginning of modern times; . . . the condemnation of Galileo and the measures adopted as a consequence of this action, which are essentially responsible for the estrangement between the Church and the natural sciences (not yet overcome today). . . ."[3]

When Pope John Paul II apologized to Jews for the Roman Church's anti-Semitism and crimes against them, he was careful to apologize for the sins of the sons and daughters of the Catholic Church. Actually it was the popes in the Inquisition and at other times who created antagonism to Jews. In a male hierarchy, "daughters," or women, had no part in the crime. The popes, in order to preserve papal infallibility, did not acknowledge the role of popes in these sinful decisions.

Similarly, when the pope apologized to the Eastern or Orthodox churches for the decision to break with them, he used the same formula, apologizing for the sins of the sons and daughters of the Church. He was so intent on pursuing the pretense of infallibility that he blamed these sins on unnamed sons (and daughters).

Where the dogma of papal infallibility impinges directly on American democracy is at the point where American courts and legislation take positions contrary to those set forth by the papacy. At these junctures, the Church attempts to overrule, through various methods, what the majority has decided is correct and what is therefore legal. A major case in point relates to abortion, birth control, and family planning.

The conflict began in the Vatican itself with a decision by Pope John XXIII to challenge the church's previous policy against birth control in the 1930 encyclical, *Casti Connubii*. He died before he could implement this, but his successor, Pope Paul VI, appointed a two-tiered commission of fifteen cardinals and bishops and a group of sixty-four lay experts from a variety of disciplines, which met from 1964 to 1966. According to Thomas Burch, a member of the commission and a professor at Georgetown University, Pope Paul VI asked the commission to find a way to change the Church's position opposing birth control without damaging papal authority.[4]

Following their two-year study, the lay commission voted 60 to 4 and the clergy 9 to 6 to change the papal teaching on birth control. The minority report, prepared chiefly by Karol Wojtyla, who became Pope John Paul II, stated in part,

> If it should be declared that contraception is not evil in itself, then we should have to concede frankly that the Holy Spirit had been on the side of the Protestant churches in 1930 [when the encyclical *Casti Connubii* was promulgated], in 1951 [Pius XII's address to the midwives], and in 1958 [the address delivered before the Society of Hematologists in the year before the pope died]. It should likewise have to be admitted that for half a century the Spirit failed to protect Pius XI, Pius XII, and a large part of the Catholic hierarchy from a very serious error. This would mean that the leaders of the Church, acting with extreme imprudence, had condemned thousands

of innocent human acts, forbidding, under pain of eternal damnation, a practice which would now be sanctioned. The fact can neither be denied nor ignored that these same acts would now be declared licit on the grounds of principle cited by the Protestants, which popes and bishops have either condemned or at least not approved.

This minority report, cited in *How the Pope Became Infallible,* by Catholic theologian A. B. Hasler, carried the conclusion by Dr. Hasler, "Thus, it became only too clear that the core of the problem was not the pill, but the authority, continuity and infallibility of the Church's magisterium."[5] Thus, Pope Paul VI accepted the minority report and wrote the encyclical *Humanae Vitae,* which is the continuing basis for the Vatican position opposing abortion and birth control.

The problem for American democracy is not merely the decision to outlaw birth control and family planning for Catholics, but the drive to impose the Vatican position, on abortion as well as a variety of other topics, on all Americans.

The papal position is also one of asserting that every sexual act must be open to procreation and hence that any sexual relation is an implied contract for pregnancy.[6] This further means that a woman, whether from a failed contraceptive or from nonuse of contraceptives, must become or remain pregnant even against her will. Compulsory pregnancy is, therefore, a form of slavery. It may aggravate a woman's serious health problems, drastically affect her work and income, and hence endanger the stability of her family and existing children. It is, therefore, also a method of controlling or subordinating women to papal dogma, as well as an exercise in papal power.

This was clearly set forth by Michael Schwartz in *Persistent Prejudice: Anti-Catholicism in America:*

> The abortion issue is the great crisis of Catholicism in the United States, of far greater import than the election of a Catholic president or the winning of tax support for Catholic education. In the unlikely event that the Church's resistance to abortion collapses and the Catholic community decides to seek an accommodation with the institutionalized killing of innocent human beings, that would signal the utter failure of Catholicism in America. It would mean that U.S. Catholics will have been defeated and denatured by the anti-Catholic host culture.[7]

The American bishops spearheaded the papal campaign in the United States against abortion and contraceptive birth control when they launched their "Pastoral Plan for Pro-Life Activities" on November 20, 1975. Since there was no biblical basis for their position on abortion, the bishops relied exclusively on papal rationales, using such phrases as, "the sanctity of life from conception onwards," and "the Church has a unique responsibility to transmit the teaching of Christ with regard to abortion and should show that abortion is a violation of God's laws."[8]

It is a papal fabrication to indicate that the Church's dogma about abortion is "the teaching of Christ." There is no reference in the New Testament to such teaching. More-over, the Vatican's idea that human life begins with concep-tion is an attempt to override the biblical position that human life begins with breathing. The Hebrew word that describes a human being is *nephesh*, the breathing one. It occurs 775 times in the Hebrew Bible. In Hebrew thought, an embryo or fetus is not a living human being because it does not breathe on its own.

There is no reference in the Bible to the sanctity or sacredness of either human or fetal life. In 2 Kings 15:16 there is reference to an order to smite all the people of a cer-tain region "and all the women therein that were with child [are to be] ripped up." Hos. 13:16 says, "their infants shall be dashed in pieces, and their women with child shall be ripped up." When Isaiah seeks vengeance against Babylon, he asks God to see that "Everyone that is found shall be thrust through . . . and they shall have no pity on the fruit of the womb; their eye shall not spare children" (Isa. 13:15–18). The separate reference to the fruit of the womb is to fetal life; it is differentiated from children. These are not isolated references to violent abortion; others can be found in Amos 2:9; Ps. 21:10; Deut. 33:11, and elsewhere.

There are also three leading biblical figures who wished for an abortion or miscarriage. Job laments (3:16), "Why was I not as a hidden untimely birth, as infants that never see the light?" Jeremiah (20:14–18) wishes he had been killed in his mother's womb. Hosea (9:14) asked God to "give them [the Israelites] a miscarrying womb and dry breasts."

Jesus, speaking of expected endtime events, showed no special concern for fetal life. He said: "Alas for those that are with child, and those that give suck in those days" (Matt. 24:19, Mark 13:11, Luke 21:23). In Luke 23:29 he said the days are coming when they will say, "blessed are the barren and wombs that never bore, and the breasts that never gave suck."

Pro-life groups mistakenly apply one of the ten commandments, "You shall not kill," to a fetus. That commandment did not refer to animals, as Israelites killed to eat and to sacrifice. It did not apply to their enemies in war and it did not even apply to all Israelites because anyone who cursed his father or mother was to be killed (Exod. 21:17). It is desperation that makes "pro-lifers" apply it to an embryo or fetus because there is no explicit reference in the entire bible that is either anti-abortion or pro-life with respect to a fetus.

If one examines Vatican dogma, it is only fetuses that have a "right to life." The pregnant woman whose life or health is endangered by the fetus has no right to life. In other words, a pregnant woman cannot save her own life by terminating the pregnancy. Over the centuries the Vatican has been involved in the direct or indirect slaughter of millions of people, including its enemies in the Crusades; the heretics and Jews in the Holy Inquisition; Protestants in the religious wars in Europe; Moors driven out of Spain; Muslims driven out of Eastern Europe by Polish-led armies; Jews, Gypsies and Communists in World War II; Serbs, Orthodox, and Muslims killed by the Croatian Ustashi Catholics during the 1930s and 1940s.

If it is argued by the pro-life movement that the Vatican has changed in recent years, it is only necessary to note that since 1975 when the bishops wrote their pro-life pastoral, the Vatican has been involved with its Maronite militia in

Lebanon. The Maronites, an Arabic-speaking group in Lebanon, have been a part of the Roman Catholic Church for centuries. They have a military force which the Vatican has assisted by providing for its training. Another example, the murder of thousands of suspected communists and political dissidents by Argentina's militia forces with the support of the Catholic hierarchy, is described by Emilio F. Mignone, a Roman Catholic, in his book *Witness to Truth: The Complicity of Church and Dictatorship in Argentina.*[9]

Moreover, to show his devotion to "life," Pope John Paul II on April 21, 1986, raised the twenty-nine Catholic military vicariates around the world to the status of dioceses. A vicariate has military jurisdiction and is governed by prelates with the same rights and privileges as a bishops. It was the military vicars in Argentina who gave the Church's approval for the military coup of March 24, 1976, that led to the murders in the subsequent "dirty war" in that country. There are at least twelve such vicariates in the Americas, including the United States, nine in Europe, three in Asia, three in Africa, and two in Oceania. The pope also insisted, against the initial vote of the U.S. bishops, on preserving the right to use nuclear weapons through the preservation of the doctrine of deterrence.

It is thus obvious that the phrase "pro-life" refers only to embryos and fetuses and not to living human beings who incur the ill will of the Vatican from time to time. At the very least it has turned a blind eye to the murder of those who would not support Catholic policies in South America and other countries. The Vatican has institutionalized militarism within its own organization. It goes to great lengths to prevent nations and the United Nations from saving the health and lives of women through family planning, birth control, and legalized abortion.

In the United States the Vatican has convinced the Christian Coalition, Focus on the Family, the Mormons, the Southern Baptist Convention, and some other Protestants to accept pro-life papal theology. Together these groups have prevailed upon the Republican Party to write Vatican theology into the Republican Party platform as follows: "The unborn child has a fundamental right-to-life that cannot be infringed."[10] This means that men and fetuses have a right to life at all times, but women lose that right when they become pregnant.

The Vatican has also announced a move that will strengthen its influence in the United States. According to a July 23, 1997, report in the *Washington Times,* Pope John Paul II was planning construction of a Pope John Paul II Cultural Center at a cost of $50 million in Washington, D.C., adjacent to the "National Shrine of the Immaculate Conception." Construction of the 100,000-square-foot center has been financed by a Detroit foundation. Planning for this Catholic Center was underway for about ten years and the center finally opened March 22, 2001.

The key to the purpose of this center is found in its focus on the teachings of the current pope and on such issues as abortion, birth control, euthanasia, assisted suicide, and ordination of women. It is described as "part interactive museum and part think tank." In other words, "it is intended to be akin to a presidential museum for the pope," and also a right-wing propaganda agency to supplement the already

Catholic-led Heritage Foundation, National Empowerment Television, and Free Congress Foundation. These have been promoting right-wing Vatican ideology in the American political sphere ever since Paul Weyrich founded them. Weyrich turned over the leadership of National Empowerment Television to William Bennett of the right-wing "Catholic Campaign for America." Bennett is former secretary of education under President Reagan and a leading advocate of vouchers for private schools.

The *Washington Times* (July 23, 1997) reported that Detroit's Cardinal Adam Maida said the pope wanted this memorial in Washington. The *Times* did not speculate about a pope who would build such a memorial to himself instead of using such funds for issues like eliminating poverty, war, disease, and other forms of injustice.

It is clear not only from the papal effort to impose its dogma on abortion and contraception in the United States but from its entire effort to achieve theocratic dominance that the problem of contraception as well as all other papal doctrine depends on the dogma of infallibility. According to Hans Küng, "The only way to solve the problem of contraception is to solve the problem of infallibility."[11]

Pope John Paul II went further in claiming that the entire foundation of Catholicism is built on infallibility. He wrote to the German Bishops Conference May 15, 1980, "I am convinced that the doctrine of infallibility is in a certain sense the key to the certainty with which the faith is confessed and proclaimed, as well as to the life and conduct of the faithful. For once this essential foundation is shaken or destroyed, the most basic truths of our faith likewise begin to break down."[12]

Such a statement can be made only if there were virtually nothing of value in the Roman Catholic faith except what must be coerced or demanded as belief. This, of course, is not true, as most of the world's great religions thrive from voluntary acceptance of religious doctrines. The pope's statement does, however, illustrate how clearly and inextricably the papacy and the Vatican view the Catholic faith in terms of power over, rather than influence with, people.

Papal insistence on infallibility, particularly with respect to contraception, also illustrates Vatican conflict with modern science, especially the various scientific findings about the amount of arable land and water available to sustain the steady increase in population in many parts of the world. The Vatican is quite prepared to insist on infallibility even in the face of vast economic migrations in search of food and water, large-scale poverty, the suffering and death of hundreds of thousands of women who have no access to contraceptives and safe legal abortion, and the starvation and death of children who cannot be given adequate food or health care. Insofar as the Vatican determines American policies with respect to family planning worldwide, it and those who implement the policies in electing legislators and appointing judges and other government officials, participate in damaging or nullifying the well-being of millions.

8

THE HIERARCHY'S INFLUENCE ON PRESIDENTIAL DECISIONS

O ne of the most important ways the Catholic hierarchy in the United States has influenced and changed public policy is through direct meetings with presidents and presidential candidates. With few exceptions, these meetings have been secret, known only to Catholic writers or kept unpublicized by an intimidated secular press. These meetings have occurred chiefly because the cardinals and bishops have created the illusion that they control the votes of American Catholics and can deliver those votes to presidential candidates who accept Vatican policies. Only one presidential candidate, as later indicated, demonstrated that the illusion has no basis in reality: Most American Catholics do not let the Vatican or its appointed bishops determine their vote.

President Ronald Reagan, who appointed Robert Reilly as his White House liaison to Roman Catholic leaders, stayed in regular touch with New York's Cardinal John J.

O'Connor. "There's a natural alliance between the [then] archbishop and the President on a goodly number of religious issues," Reilly told a reporter.[1] That alliance was not merely the fact that O'Connor had registered as a Republican in October 1980, during Reagan's presidential campaign, or that O'Connor and Reagan shared an opposition to abortion; they also shared military convictions. "O'Connor was chaplain for the first Marine ground forces in Vietnam in 1965" and "like the President, defended American war aims in Vietnam. 'The chaplain's job,' he said in one of his first interviews as Archbishop, 'is to teach people to love even if you have to kill.'"[2] According to the *Village Voice* newspaper, "The Archbishop and the President are willing to make more exceptions for the moral use of nuclear weapons from limited war to a first strike policy, than they are for raped women in search of an abortion."[3]

O'Connor was also involved with the Reagan administration in the opposition to the Sandinista government in Nicaragua, and in attacking Geraldine Ferraro, the Democratic candidate for vice president on the team opposing Reagan's reelection in 1984.[4]

O'Connor was not alone in assisting and influencing Reagan. Philadelphia's Cardinal John Kroll praised the president in a campaign stop at the Polish-American Catholic shrine in Doylestown, Pennsylvania, and delivered the invocation the night Reagan was nominated for re-election at the Republican national convention. O'Connor was at one time a diocesan priest in Kroll's archdiocese, and Kroll had recommended O'Connor to Pope John Paul II for the position of cardinal.[5]

Moreover, after Reagan announced that the United States would establish diplomatic relations with the Vatican, the pope's representative, Archbishop Pio Laghi, "took a $16,000 plane ride thanks to the President, who'd summoned him in August from Washington for a West Coast meeting. Laghi [also] took a 14 passenger C-20 gratis to the Virgin Islands after his visit with the President," which says "something about the relationship of the pope and the president."[6]

Also during the Reagan administration, the Central Intelligence Agency (C.I.A.) collaborated with Pope John Paul II, who got "frequent C.I.A. briefings. C.I.A. detectors geared to warn against terrorist attack from the air, have been installed on the roof of the papal apartment. . . . Security agents provided by the C.I.A. supposedly accompanied the pope to Nicaragua, where he took on the Sandinistas. The C.I.A., through the American embassy in Warsaw, kept John Paul informed of Soviet reaction during his historic visit to Poland."[7]

There is much more. For example, Ana Maria Escurra in her book *The Vatican and the Reagan Administration* notes that the Reagan administration provided financial support from the Agency for International Development—a well-known official institution of the United States—to the Archdiocese of Managua, in Nicaragua, which pursued Vatican policies in Central America that coincided with Reagan's.[8]

Reagan was not the only president who followed the lead of the Catholic bishops. In his book, *Catholic Bishops in American Politics*, Timothy Byrnes describes the American bishops' approach to presidential candidate Jimmy Carter. "The key figure in these backchannel communications between the Catholic Conference and Carter's campaign was Bishop James Rausch. Rausch was, in effect, chief of staff of the entire National Conference of Catholic Bishops (NCCB)/United States Catholic Conference bureaucracy."[9] After a number of informal contacts Rausch had through emissaries to Carter and a personal meeting with Walter Mondale, Carter's vice presidential candidate, Rausch and Carter campaign officials decided to arrange a personal meeting between Carter and the leaders of the bishops' conference. At such a meeting they decided a whole range of issues could be discussed. [10] Archbishop Joseph L. Bernardin led the executive committee of the National Conference of Catholic Bishops that met with Carter August 31, 1976, at the Mayflower Hotel in Washington.[11]

At the Mayflower Hotel meeting, one of the major agreements was subsequently revealed by R. T. Ravenholt, M.D., who directed the population program of the U.S. Agency for International Development (AID) in the State Department from 1966 to 1979. In an address in Seattle on March 4, 1991, to the state branch of Zero Population Growth, Ravenholt described both the effort of congressional Catholics to "fire Ravenholt" and the deal Carter made with the bishops. Ravenholt said the bishops pressed Carter "to de-emphasize federal support for family planning in exchange for a modicum of Catholic support for his presidential race," and subsequently "President-elect Carter proceeded to put the two federal agencies with family planning programs under Catholic control.[12]

Thus, Joseph Califano, a Catholic, became Secretary of Health, Education, and Welfare. Dr. Ravenholt also revealed that "a longtime Catholic adversary of AID's family planning program, John H. Sullivan, moved from Congressman Clement Zablocki's office into AID during the presidential transition and was given a key role in selecting Carter's political appointees. . . . In 1973, Jack Sullivan and allied zealots helped Senator Jesse Helms develop the Helms Amendment to the Foreign Assistance Act. Since then this amendment has prevented AID from providing assistance for the termination of unwanted pregnancies."[13]

Ravenholt continued, "In hearings of the House Foreign Affairs Committee on July 18, 1975, Zablocki stated for the record his antipathy to contraceptives and discussed with a right-to-life representative, Randy Engel, the removal of Dr. Ravenholt. 'I would hope that we could find a way of removing him.'"[14] Dr. Ravenholt was subsequently removed.

Ravenholt also reported other religious initiatives to curb birth control and family planning programs. He said, "According to members of the Food and Drug Administration (FDA) Committee on Obstetrics, in 1978, after the FDA already had informed the Upjohn Company that its product, Depo Provera, was approvable, it was HEW Secretary Joseph Califano who specifically directed that FDA not approve Depo Provera for marketing as a contraceptive"[15]

In the meantime, Gerald Ford, who was president from 1974 to 1977 and was Carter's opponent in 1976, also succumbed to the Catholic bishops' influence. According to Byrnes, Ford not only acquiesced in an antiabortion plank in the Republican platform and spoke to a Catholic Eucharistic Congress in Philadelphia, but invited Archbishop Joseph Bernardin and the other members of the executive committee to meet with him at the White House, where "Ford, like Carter, assured the bishops that he shared their moral opposition to abortion."[16]

Nevertheless, the bishops did not actually endorse either Carter or Ford, but were in a position to take credit and extend their influence over the winning candidate.

We have already referred to President Reagan's close relation to the Vatican and its influence on American policy. His successor, George H. W. Bush, was also responsive to the hierarchy. Doug Wead, special assistant to Bush, in an interview with the *National Catholic Reporter*, said of Bush, "He has been more sensitive and more accessible to the needs of the Catholic Church than any president I know of in American history." He also said, "We want the Church to feel loved and wanted, and we want them to have input."[17]

By "the Church" Bush meant the official church—the cardinals and bishops—rather than the Catholic people. Wead noted, "This administration has appointed more Catholic cabinet officers than any other in American history."[18]

Dr. Stephen Mumford, president of the Center for Research on Population and Security, reported, "Within a month after Bush became President, all five of the cardinals had been included in meetings in the Bush family quarters. Both Law and O'Connor spent at least one overnight at the White House as guests of the President."[19]

When it was clear that Bush would be a candidate for re-election, O'Connor, now a cardinal, endorsed Bush. "Accompanied by John Cardinal O'Connor, Mr. Bush appeared before a wildly applauding flag-waving crowd at a Knights of Columbus meeting in New York to present himself as the nation's 'moral compass.'"[20] Mumford also asserted that "during the Carter-Reagan-Bush years, the bishops directed an infiltration of every U.S. government office and agency that has anything to do with family planning, abortion, immigration and population growth control."[21]

During Bush's term in office, the Earth Summit took place in Rio de Janeiro in June 1992, for which the Vatican began "a campaign to try to insure that the gathering's conclusions are not in conflict with Roman Catholic teaching on birth control."[22] Bush supported the Vatican.

One of the most respected U.S. environmental organizations, the Sierra Club, in a July 9, 1992, release attacked President Bush for vetoing "two foreign aid budgets in order to block all U.S. funding for the United Nations Fund for Population Activities." The Sierra Club noted that the United States was the only major country not to fund the UN's population program.[23] The Sierra Club not only linked President Bush's policy to the Vatican's influence but also asserted that during President Bush's four years in office, 52 million children under the age of five died, many of them from preventable diseases, and noted that, "Some 399 million couples are without access to family planning services."[24] In light of the well-known Vatican opposition to birth control, it is not surprising that Bush won endorsement of Cardinal O'Connor and others in the hierarchy.

When William Jefferson Clinton ran for the presidency in 1992, he appealed directly to progressive Catholics rather than to the bishops. During his first term, Clinton supported birth control measures and vetoed a measure that would ban late term abortions known medically as intact dilation and evacuation (D&E) but which the bishops called "partial birth" abortions or "infanticides." Clinton had urged Congress to recognize the health of the mother, not only a threat of her death, as a basis for exception. The bishops, however, with their right-to-life movement, saw this as an opportunity to create public criticism of Clinton. Eight U.S.-based cardinals demonstrated on the Capitol steps in Washington on September 12, 1996, in an unusual political action to urge Congress to override President Clinton's veto.[25] Prior to the House vote an advertisement was repeatedly shown on TV that did not reveal the real sponsors but claimed to be an unnamed ad hoc physicians' group against "partial birth abortions."

The only major Catholic voice supporting Clinton's veto was Rev. Robert F. Drinan, a Jesuit priest on the Georgetown University faculty. He wrote, "Had the measure he vetoed become law, it would have meant that obstetricians could be charged with a federal crime if they performed a late abortion by the one legally forbidden technique. . . . As a result, the small number of abortions done after 20 weeks of pregnancy would be done by other methods that are statistically less safe. . . . It does not make sense for a federal law, for the first time in history, to enter into such a complicated arena of specialized professional and ethical issues."[26]

Thus, during the presidential campaign of 1996 between Clinton and Robert Dole, the president of the NCCB, Anthony M. Pilla of Cleveland, departed from custom to tell the 250 bishops that, although they should not engage in partisan politics, they could address political issues that might be closer to the views of one party. Then, after a

"stinging" attack on President Clinton's veto of the intact
D&E late-term abortions, the bishops (according to the June
24, 1996, *New York Times*) unanimously endorsed Dole's
appeal to Congress to overturn the veto.

The *New York Times* also reported that orders had been
placed by the Conference of Bishops for more than nine million sets of postcards to be sent by constituents to their legislators urging Congress to overturn the veto. This political
campaign obviously made the bishops' political position felt
throughout the country. On no issue other than abortion
and birth control have the bishops been so openly political.

Just before the November election, an advertisement was
run on numerous TV stations throughout the United States
which obviously had the support of the bishops, though for
tax and legal reasons it was sponsored by "The United States
Catholic Coalition," which did not exist, prior to or following the TV ad series, in any published list of church
organizations. Following is the transcript and description of
the spot, which instructs Catholics that they cannot vote for
"pro-abortion" candidates:

> Scene 1 —Roman Catholic priest Fr. Lawrence
> Battle in black suit seated at a table with a crucifix
> to his right, with a plain blue background. He is
> holding an open copy of the "CATECHISM OF
> THE CATHOLIC CHURCH." Fr. Battle speaks
> directly to the viewer: "I am Father Battle. It is the
> mission of the Catholic Church to pass moral
> judgments in matters related to politics whenever
> the fundamental rights of man requires it."
> Scene 2—Photograph of Bill Clinton with

word "SHAME" in large boldface red letters flashing on and off diagonally across his face.

Scene 3—Graphic with "Democratic Party" at the top of the screen above the donkey logo of the Democratic Party which is below on the left. To the right are two bulleted lines reading "Abortion" and "Partial Birth Abortion."

During scene 2 and scene 3, the voice of Fr. Battle continues, "The Democratic Party and Bill Clinton have brought shame and horror to this nation. They have legalized the savage murder of babies during birth. We are outraged."

Scene 4—returns to Fr. Battle, who again speaks directly to the viewer: "Catholics must uphold human rights, avoid sin, and cannot vote for abortion candidates. Cannot vote for Clinton."

Scene 5—appears while Father Battle is finishing the above words. It is a repeat of scene 2 of the Clinton photo with the word "SHAME" in large boldface letters flashing on and off diagonally over his face. At the bottom of the screen are the words in small type, "Paid for by the United States Catholic Coalition."

Music: During the entire 30 second spot, Mozart's *Requiem* can be heard softly in the background, with the volume level swelling up toward the end of the spot.[27]

Legal Counsel for the National Right to Life Committee in Washington (the official organization which has the confidence of the National Council of Catholic Bishops [NCCB]) advised that "Pastors and churches are free to discuss the positions of candidates on issues . . . including criticizing or praising them for their positions. The endorsement of a candidate includes any statement which uses explicit words to expressly advocate the election or defeat of candidates. A church may not engage in such advocacy but a pastor in his individual capacity may."

Despite its most overt attempt to control the outcome of a presidential election, the hierarchy was unable to elect Bob Dole. Many American Catholics, as much as other Americans, may have been offended by such smear tactics as the "Shame" ad attacking Clinton. However, the various political activities of the American bishops reveal how deeply involved the Vatican and its agents are in American politics, how clearly they influence the political process, and how tough their opposition becomes when political leaders do not submit to their control.

The Vatican also directly criticizes U.S. officials who depart from Vatican control. Columnist William Safire, referring to the Vatican's public attack on Vice President Al Gore, who represented the United States at the Cairo Conference, said, "The Pope's representative impugned the sincerity of Gore's conciliatory assertion that the U.S. did not seek an international right to abortion. . . . That was a personal insult issued in the Pope's name. Unless corrected, it will stand as unprecedented papal meddling in U.S. politics." Safire also condemned Bishop James McHugh's effort to "predict the political behavior of co-religionists" as McHugh did "with his warning of a powerful incentive to American Catholics to walk away from the Democratic Party."[28]

In addition to trying to control the president and his

administration, the Catholic bishops are active in state politics. In Missouri, for example, Catholic lobbyists not only oppose abortion but all family planning. One of their lobbyists said, "Planned Parenthood, by the very nature of what they do, should not get funds" even though Planned Parenthood uses only private contributions for abortion services.[29]

A columnist for the *Kansas City Star* wrote, "But all of this activity really isn't about abortion. This muscle flexing is about power. The fight over family planning funding is about revenge against Planned Parenthood, a major provider of family planning services. . . . It is a sneering attack on poor women who will be denied access to family planning services, particularly in rural areas. Clinics will close and fees for services will be higher. . . . There will also be more abortions."[30]

What the *Star* and other papers fail to mention is that the pope forbids all contraceptives and that everywhere in the world all Catholic dioceses and all bishops and cardinals must march in lock step to the orders from Rome. There is no greater evidence of totalitarianism than the fact that no bishop, priest, or other appointed official is ever free to deviate from papal orders. It is even rare for Catholic judges to deviate from the papal position. That is why the American hierarchy is working so hard to secure judicial appointments that will overthrow established court precedents that permit safe, legal abortions. The Vatican is concerned with power, not only over its own constituents, but over government at every level.

9

SOME FALLIBLE ACTS OF INFALLIBLE POPES

Infallibility: The dogma that the Pope, as the Supreme Pontiff, is divinely guarded from error when speaking officially on matters of faith or of morals. (Webster's New Universal Unabridged Dictionary, *2d ed.)*

The papal doctrine of infallibility was promulgated in 1870 by the First Vatican Council at the insistence of Pope Pius IX.[1] However, it was not suddenly discovered, for, as Pius IX elaborated, it is a "tradition received from the beginning of the Christian faith."[2] This of course is not true, for there is nothing in the New Testament or the early churches to support it.

The "infallibility" of popes generally applies to a pope's decrees about faith and morals. But he can stretch the term "morals" to cover any act he chooses, even if rational judgment of others see it as an immoral act. It is very difficult, therefore, to differentiate between moral decisions and those which are open to human error. All papal actions are subject to rational criticism, even if the Vatican claims otherwise.

It is not logically possible to claim that the pope is the vicar of Christ receiving revelation directly from God and at the same time label only some of his acts as infallible, as he does. In any event, history records the serious errors of many "infallible" popes. For example, it was the actions of the early popes, Innocent I (402–417), Leo I (440–461), Felix III (483–492), and Gregory (590–601) which led to the schism between the Eastern and the Roman Catholic churches.[3]

A second major mistake was the Crusades. Although Jerusalem had been in Muslim possession since 638, pilgrimages of Christians to the Holy Land except for brief intervals continued practically uninterrupted. The conquest of Jerusalem by the Seljuk Turks led to an appeal from the Eastern Empire to Rome, and in 1095 Pope Urban II called for a holy war against the Muslims which lasted for centuries. The popes lost the Holy Land but did control Constantinople, where the Eastern or Greek Church was "made subject to the Pope. . . . This Latin conquest was disastrous. It greatly weakened the Eastern empire and augmented the hatred between Greek and Latin Christianity."[4]

In 1209 Pope Innocent III directed a bloody crusade against the Albigensians, a religious sect in southern France, declaring them heretics, marking the birth of the Inquisition.[5]

Pope Paul III in 1542 began the Roman Inquisition in Italy against heretics. Galileo (1564–1642), the great Italian astronomer and physicist, was among its victims. In Italy, under the impetus of Pope Paul IV (1555–1559), the Inquisition helped to eliminate the Protestants.[6] The Spanish Inquisition "was organized by the Dominican Tomas de Torquemada (1420–1498) and confirmed by the Pope." Its victims numbered in the thousands; about 2,000 were burned to death. Most of them were Jews or Muslims who had been converted to Christianity but were suspected of maintaining or relapsing into their earlier faith.[7] The papal assumption in authorizing the Inquisition was that disbelief must be punished. Even torture was introduced by Pope Innocent IV.[8]

In more modern times the popes and their agents have continued to make serious errors that one would reasonably consider to have been impossible for them to make had they been infallible or direct interpreters of God's will. On December 20, 1926, Pope Pius XI declared that Benito Mussolini, the fascist dictator of Italy, was "the man sent by Providence," and in the United States the bishop of Cleveland called him the "Man of Destiny," while Cardinal O'Connell of Boston, who had received a high fascist decoration, exalted him as "a genius in the field of government given to Italy by God." The pope signed a Concordat and Lateran Treaty with Mussolini on February 11, 1929, discriminating against Jews and Protestants and establishing "the Catholic Apostolic and Roman religion as the sole religion of the state."[9] The Lateran Treaty opened the way for Vatican approval of Mussolini's war against Ethiopia.

In Spain the fascist dictator Francisco Franco made Catholicism the official religion and received the support of the Spanish Church hierarchy and also the American hierarchy.[10]

There were similar relations between the Vatican and the Catholic dictator in Portugal, Antonio Salazar. The Concordat of 1940 between Portugal and the Vatican provided for aid to Catholic schools and other measures that gave the Roman church a privileged status, such as a monopoly of missions in Portuguese colonies.[11]

Hitler was also acceptable to Rome. The Concordat was continued, as were diplomatic relations, and the Nazi control of Catholic Austria and Czechoslovakia was accepted. When France was conquered by Germany, the Vatican supported the Vichy regime under Henri Philippe Petain instead of the resistance movement against the Nazis.[12]

Throughout the Fascist period the Vatican and its agents, the cardinals and bishops, accepted anti-Semitism, including the persecution and extermination of Jews during the Holocaust. It was not until 1997—more than fifty years after the fact—that the French bishops finally apologized for their failure to oppose anti-Jewish laws in 1940 and for the deportation of more than 75,000 Jews to Nazi death camps.[13] When the Germans occupied Rome in September 1943, Jews were rounded up and taken to a temporary jail "only two hundred yards from Vatican City," but "from the Vatican no voice was raised in public support of the Jews," according to James Carroll, an ex-priest.[14]

Carroll, not content with the accusation of silence, refers to Harvard professor Daniel Jonah Goldhagen's 1996 book, *Hitler's Willing Executioners*, which indicates that Christian churches in Germany supplied crucial records to the Nazis detailing Jewish descent, thereby abetting in the Nazi atrocities.

Carroll asked Hans Küng whether the absolutism with which the Church defends this tradition reduces infallibility to the absurd. "Yes," Küng replied, "Exactly."

Carroll also notes the centuries of anti-Semitism on the part of the Church that set the stage for the Holocaust; and the current insistence "upon the primacy of Jesus as a means of salvation, and upon the Church as 'the absolute religion' which remains the ground even of much Catholic ecumenism." Carroll refers to the cross, often "used as a sign of conquest," and "religion as a source of brutality." He quotes a Catholic theologian, Padraic O'Hara, as saying, "Universalist absolutism thrives on the diminishment of the other."[15]

Although these events further demonstrate the fallibility of the "infallible" popes, another catastrophe is in the making because of papal dictates in the name of morality. The United Nations Fund for Population Activities (UNFPA) in 1991 said, "World population, which reached 5.4 billion in mid-1991, is growing faster than ever before: three people every second, more than 250,000 every day. At the beginning of the decade the annual addition was 93 million; by the end it will approach 100 million. At this rate the world will have almost a billion more people (roughly the population of China) by the year 2001."[16]

So urgent is the slowing of population growth that a joint statement was issued shortly thereafter by the officers of the Royal Society of London and the National Academy of Sciences of the United States which in summary stated, "If current predictions of population growth prove accurate and patterns of human activity on the planet remain unchanged, science and technology may not be able to prevent either irreversible degradation of the environment or continued poverty for much of the world."[17] However, an organization more powerful than any of these international groups has used its influence with major governments to prevent discussion of overpopulation and funding of family planning programs. The *New York Times* reported on May 28, 1992, "In preparation for next month's Earth Summit in

Rio de Janeiro, Vatican diplomats have begun a campaign to try to insure that the gathering's conclusions on the issue of runaway population growth are not in conflict with Roman Catholic teaching on birth control." According to the same report, "officials said Vatican diplomats insisted on changing the wording in references to 'family planning' to the formulation: 'the responsible planning of family size in keeping with fundamental dignity and personally held values and taking into account ethical and cultural considerations.'"[18]

This "more cumbersome wording," said the *Times*, "reflects the Roman Catholic Church's prohibition on all forms of artificial birth control."[19]

In order to defend papal doctrines against family planning, contraception, and also abortion, the Vatican says there is enough arable land and food potential to feed ever larger populations. The problem is not only land, but all natural resources. For example, fresh water is limited. "People withdraw the equivalent of Lake Huron from the world's rivers, streams, lakes and aquifers each year, and withdrawals have been increasing four to eight percent a year in recent decades. . . . Supplies of water are beginning to fall behind demand in northern China and the World Resources Institute says shortages could reach crisis proportions in the Middle East before this decade is out. Shortages have become a familiar and serious problem in the southwestern United States, particularly in California."[20]

The shortage of water in the Mideast is illustrative. "No matter what progress irrigated agriculture makes, Jordan's natural water at this pace will be exhausted in 2010," predicted Elias Salameh, founder and former director of the

University of Jordan's Water Research and Study Center. "Jordan then will be totally dependent on rain water and will revert to desert. Its ruin will destabilize the entire region."[21] Salameh continued, "None of the regional countries—Egypt, Israel, Jordan, Syria, Saudi Arabia or the Gulf Emirates—can be self-sufficient in food in the foreseeable future, if ever. All Middle East economies must be restructured away from agriculture because of a lack of water."[22]

In southern Africa "eleven countries with a population of more than 120 million are living under a drought previously unknown to the region in its sweep and severity. . . . Lakes have dried up. . . . 17 million people are now under direct threat of starvation."[23]

Humans also use other indispensable resources: "The population explosion in the developing countries has intensified the pressure on forests . . . which are one of the last sources of fuel and of new pasture and arable land, however marginal. . . . As a result, according to United Nations estimates, an area of tropical forest larger than the state of Florida is disappearing each year. . . . Worldwide, scientists say there has been a net loss of more than 3 million square miles of forest, an area roughly equal to the 48 contiguous states of the United States. About half the loss has come since 1850."[24] Trees play a vital role in the maintenance of the biosphere. They hold soil in place, "preventing erosion and the silting of rivers. They absorb vast amounts of heat trapping carbon dioxide and lock it up in their cells."[25] They produce oxygen required for human and all other animal life.

There is little question that Vatican dogma against family planning is a factor in the population crisis. The pope travels throughout Africa, Latin America, and other parts of the world condemning birth control and family planning. Reducing the rate of population growth through contraception that lowers the birth rate will ease the strain on the environment and lead to an increase in the quality of human life. Therefore Vatican dogma jeopardizes all of humanity.

There are numerous other mistakes made by the Vatican, including the ban on abortion even to save the health or life of the woman; the assumption that the role of women is that of housewife and mother; the ban on women serving as priests when they have served the church as nuns and in other capacities for centuries; the ban on homosexuality when many gays and lesbians have served unostentatiously in a celibate ministry for centuries, even when the American Medical Association and American Psychiatric Association have called for a nonjudgmental recognition of persons of different sexual orientations.

The celibate priesthood requirement itself is another costly mistake. National Public Radio in 1997 reported that the American Church had paid out $650 million because of sexual abuse of parishioners by priests.[26] A related 1997 story referred to well-publicized illicit relationships of priests who have acknowledged fathering children, but also said that unfortunately, some have quietly arranged for abortions, often with the knowledge of their bishops.[27]

An Episcopal bishop, the Rt. Rev. John M. Spong, writing about the "unwillingness of the Roman Catholic Church to allow dissent about great theological issues," provided this summary:

Rome did not open itself to the field of Biblical scholarship until well after World War II. The antiquated idea of Papal infallibility in the defining of faith and morals continues to make learned dialogue with any nonconforming ideas all but impossible. . . . I am embarrassed that a branch of the Christian Church as recently as the late 1940s, in an encyclical by Pope Pius XII, was still denying the insights of Charles Darwin. I ache for Roman Catholic scholars who have to compromise their scholarly findings in order to receive the church's imprimatur. I feel the pain of Hans Küng, a deeply devoted Roman Catholic priest and professor, who was removed from his chair as a Roman Catholic theologian at Tubingen, and the pain of Charles Curran who was removed from his tenured position at Catholic University because neither of these Roman Catholic priests could as scholars affirm the present Catholic position as interpreted by Joseph Cardinal Ratzinger. I stare in amazement at the ecclesiastical attempts at mind control that will stoop to silence Matthew Fox and Leonardo Boff.

I wonder whence comes the fear that is expressed in refusing to entertain new ideas? Sigmund Freud once suggested that any system of thought that claims to have been received by divine revelation against which there is no appeal, that is dispensed to the people through the only body that was authorized to receive that revelation and which claims infallibility for its articulation of that revelation and, therefore, allows no challenges and no questions, is clearly a system of thought that its adherents do not really believe. Truth that is really believed does not have to be so deeply protected from honest inquiry. But religious propaganda designed to enhance institutional power always requires protection. Why, one must ask, is any religious organization afraid of its own people and its own scholars? Why is it afraid of open inquiry? Or, as one religious poster once observed, why is it that churches that claim to have all the answers will not allow any questions?[28]

10

GOVERNMENT FUNDING FOR SEGREGATED EDUCATION

T he privatization of education with the support of funds taken from the public school budget has long been a goal of some religious and secular groups. Protestant churches and the Jewish community ordinarily support separation of church and state and support public schools. Various groups that operate private schools, such as the Episcopalians, Quakers, Mennonites, Seventh-day Adventists, and the elite "prep" schools, have not sought public funding or joined a movement to subvert public education. The term "school choice," however, has recently been used to describe the position that parents should be able to send their children to private schools with public assistance. Legislation to authorize such public funding would provide for vouchers or tuition tax credits which parents could take to a private school and the school in turn would seek government reimbursement.

A voucher is a device by which authority to use public funds would be conveyed through certificates given to parents in an effort to circumvent federal and state constitutional prohibitions against government funding of religious institutions. The government agency would transmit the money from public funds directly to the school that collected the voucher.

The early proposals for vouchers came from advocates of government funding for parochial schools. The October 25, 1957, *U.S. News & World Report* said that Father Virgil C. Blum, S.J., of Marquette University, had advocated a program of indirect aid to parochial schools which he called "the certificate or voucher plan." Blum wrote, "Under such a plan the State government gives parents of nonpublic school children certificates of money value for their children's education in the school of their choice."[1]

"Citizens for Educational Freedom" was organized in 1959 in St. Louis to lobby for the Blum plan. The Second Vatican Council's decree on Christian Education, on October 28, 1965, endorsed this concept: "Parents, who have a primary and inalienable duty and right in regard to the education of their children, should enjoy the fullest liberty in their choice of school. The public authority, therefore, whose duty it is to protect and defend the liberty of the citizens, is bound according to the principles of distributive justice to ensure that public subsidies to schools are so allocated that parents are truly free to select schools for their children in accordance with their conscience."[2]

The phrase "distributive justice" is an Aristotelian idea that superior status or contribution to society entitled one to greater benefits from that society. It was an aristocratic principle which denied benefits of Greek citizenship to slaves. The medieval world in which Roman Catholic structure, theology, and social principles were largely formed was not opposed to this idea of distribution in proportion to status.

Aristotle also used a concept known as arithmetical justice, which gives the same equally to each. This is theoretically descriptive of the American public school system, although that equality has not been reached in many cities and rural areas because of inequitable distribution of funding, poverty, and racial segregation.

The voucher program which is based on distributive justice or the concept of status would provide tax dollars chiefly to two classes of parents: those wealthy enough to send their children to the private academies of the rich, and those parents who can afford tuition for their children in parochial or other religious day schools. Although the word "justice" is used and it is argued that vouchers would aid the poor, few if any poor parents, as we shall indicate, could qualify for voucher programs.

The real push for vouchers nationally and in the states has been organized by the National Conference of Catholic Bishops. The Protestant and Catholic right-wing groups have simply adopted the position in favor of aid to religious schools long held by the Catholic bishops. The Protestant fundamentalist support can be understood by the fact that the largest recent growth of religious schools is fundamentalist and evangelical Protestant.

A study of the way a voucher program would work in Pennsylvania, based on $900 for each student in the state, revealed that (because private schools are generally located in wealthy neighborhoods) "two-thirds of the funds authorized by this plan would flow into the eight Pennsylvania counties [out of 67] with the highest per capita incomes, while none of the funds would go to the state's poorest counties." This means that the state's poorest counties would "be paying additional taxes to support the richest counties."[3]

An examination of the top fifty-one private school counties in the United States reveals similarly how tax money would flow into religious schools to the detriment of public schools in the same county and state. For example, in Carroll County, Iowa, the first of the fifty-one counties studied, where the Catholic Church population is 62.4 percent, 37.8 percent of the students are in private schools. In Sioux County, Iowa, the second highest county, where the Dutch Reformed churches are dominant, 37.4 percent of students are in private schools.[4] Membership in the Roman Catholic Church is a paramount factor in the top fifty-one counties, which range between 20.3 percent of all students to 37.8 percent in religious schools, even without a voucher program. A number of prosperous suburbs with strong Catholic identities are in the top fifty, including Jefferson County, Louisiana; the Philadelphia suburban counties of Delaware, Montgomery, and Bucks; St. Louis County, Missouri; and the Cincinnati suburban counties of Kenton and Campbell, Kentucky. There is thus often a correlation between religious schools and higher incomes.[5]

In general, large cities with historically large Catholic communities (Philadelphia, Jersey City, Boston, Wilmington, Cincinnati, Baton Rouge, Louisville, Wheeling,

Cleveland, New Orleans, and San Francisco) are among the top fifty-one counties. Voucher support of 20 to 40 percent of the student populations would mean that state taxes to support the private schools would have to come not only from the counties with high private school populations but also the counties with few, if any, private schools. The families with children in private schools would benefit substantially while those in public schools would correspondingly lose tax revenue. For example, a family with five children receiving a $3,000 tuition voucher per child or $15,000 a year would benefit enormously, while the public school family would suffer from the corresponding reduction in per-pupil aid to the public school.

The call for voucher aid to parochial and other religious schools is never preceded by a demand for more funds for public schools and their underpaid teachers. "Distributive justice" is thus a rationale for special privilege for one or more rival school systems and not an illustration of religious concern for the poor and needy of all faiths and none.

"Distributive justice" is based on the assumption that certain parents as taxpayers are being denied justice if they do not get back from the government part or all of what they pay in taxes. Taxes, of course, are not levied on parents as such. They are levied on property or income or purchases. It is a matter of parental choice not to accept the benefits provided by public schools. But taxpayers without children have no choice of schools. However, everyone in the community benefits from public schools that lift the level of education and ability to participate in our democracy.

There is also a correlation between race and private

school enrollment. In the two dozen most heavily African American counties in the nation, 11 percent of all white elementary and secondary students attended white private schools in 1990, compared to 9.8 percent average for all U.S. states. In Georgia, high private school counties had black populations higher than statewide. In Humphreys County, Mississippi, 17.9 percent of all students attended private schools, and Wilkinson County, 21.4 percent.[6] This explains why many Southern Baptist and other fundamentalist groups in the South support the Catholic voucher proposal.

No figures are immediately available to determine white flight from black areas in the large cities of the North. However, voucher programs would not only subsidize the existing racially motivated schools, but accelerate white flight.

A more recent demand for vouchers has come from some in the business community and politicians responsive to the position of the church hierarchy, but using the idea that funding private schools would provide competition that would improve public schools. These arguments are held by a small but influential minority on the basis of inadequate evidence. A 1991 report released by the Committee for Economic Development, an independent research and educational organization comprising over 250 business and education leaders, concluded that "new research into student achievement demonstrated that, by itself, choice does not guarantee educational quality. We believe that where choice systems are put into place, they should involve the public schools only."[7] (Choice within public schools refers to existing alternatives such as academic and commercial subjects, industrial arts, and, in various magnet schools, specialization in subjects such as languages, agriculture, and ecology—a wide variety of studies not available in any private religious or nonsectarian school. Public schools also have programs for disadvantaged or disabled students seldom offered in private schools.)

Money magazine (October 1994) concluded after investigation by nineteen reporters and correspondents that "Students who attend the best public schools outperform most private school students. The average public school teacher has stronger academic qualifications than the average private school teacher. The best public schools offer a more challenging curriculum than most private schools. Public school class sizes are no larger than in most private schools, and are smaller than in most Catholic schools."[8]

The assumption that education in general will improve if parents, through vouchers, are able to choose private schools has no proof. Arnold Fege of the National Parent Teachers Association wrote,

> Voucher proponents assume a cause-effect relationship between competition and quality in the marketplace and that a similar dynamic would work with schools. In business, however, the relationship between competition and quality is a function of profit. If a company can show greater profit by providing a cheaper, lower quality product or no-frills service, it will. If a service— hospitalization for the poor, or airline service to smaller communities—is not profitable, it won't be provided. A company is not in business to give the consumer the best product or service at the lowest

price but to improve its profit margin by any method that will work. Competition, then, impacts pricing far more than it does product quality.[9]

When a private firm, Education Alternatives, signed a contract in 1994 with the Hartford, Connecticut, Board of Education to manage its school system, "City officials said a company spending plan . . . that called for hundreds of staff reductions and the possibility of larger class sizes sparked a revolt by parents and teachers that could not be contained."[10]

Some argue that funding private schools would create competition which would improve public schools. This ignores the fact that competition between religious and public schools existed for decades during the many years when religious schools did not charge tuition because the churches and their religious teachers managed the cost. During those years, as well as today, large numbers of Catholic parents sent their children to public schools because of their general superiority. As James Michael Lee, editor of *Catholic Education in the Western World*, states in his chapter on Catholic education in the United States, "Broadly considered, government schools are generally superior to Catholic schools at every level, with of course many notable exceptions." Furthermore, "[g]overnment schools have always taken the lead in all spheres of professionalization, especially in experimentation, in guidance and in instructional services. Catholic schools generally have lagged behind, criticizing government schools for their innovational practices and ending up tardily accepting these improvements."[11]

There were a number of attempts to fund vouchers through federal legislation in the 1970s and 1980s, but these proposals were defeated because they were seen as elitist. Since then, an attempt to repackage the voucher idea has been one also offering vouchers to low-income families in addition to middle-class and wealthy parents. One motivation for this is the desire of politicians who want to privatize education to appeal to low-income voters. Another is the desire of some proponents of religious schools to enroll minority students who are not of their religious denomination. Thomas J. Reese, S.J., notes that "Catholic schools are the most successful evangelizing tool available to the church in the black community. . . . Most schools teach the Catholic faith to both Catholic and non-Catholic students."[12]

One illustration of this is Chicago's Holy Angels School, which President Reagan visited to propose tuition financial aid for parents to send their children to nonpublic schools. Reagan called it "the nation's largest black Catholic school" and asserted that "the people who will benefit most are the minorities and the poor." The *Washington Post* of April 12, 1981, reported that in order to attend that school both the children and their parents must be instructed in Catholicism, which meant about 80 to 150 conversions a year.

No one can question the use of church schools for the purpose of proselytizing children and parents of other faiths, but no government should directly or indirectly fund such schools with public funds extracted from all taxpayers.

However, in many cities there are few private schools available that would not proselytize children. If the only nonpublic school in a given city or county is administered by one denomination, such as the Missouri Synod Lutheran Church or the major Catholic school systems throughout the United States, there is no real voucher choice for members of other denominations who object to their theology.

Another more serious argument against the proposal of relief for low-income families is that vouchers do not pay the full cost of tuition at most private schools. One of the major additional costs is transportation, since there are almost no neighborhood private schools. If the nearest nonsectarian private school or Catholic or Lutheran high school is in the next county or across an urban area, traditional bus routes are inadequate. Taxis or twice daily car transportation would be necessary and beyond the reach of poor families.

Rich or middle-income parents can afford clothing, educational supplies, and extracurricular activities, but poor parents cannot. It is foolish to claim that vouchers would equalize educational opportunities. In states where transportation is provided for nonpublic school students, the cost to taxpayers is tremendous. In Kansas City, Missouri, which has had a modified program of school choice within its public school system, the district used up to 400 taxicabs to transport students from home to school. And in Montclair, New Jersey, "transportation expenditures have increased by approximately $1.5 million annually as a result of the 'choice' program."[13]

One of the assumptions that low-income families may gain a private school education is based on the lower tuition rates for church schools. Costs are lower at sectarian private schools because they are already partly subsidized by tax-deductible contributions. Economist Donald Frey writes that when the state introduces tuition subsidies, there will be "strong incentive to raise tuition."[14] The teachers, aware of government subsidies, will want wages comparable to public school teachers rather than to church workers.

Although taxpayers would be subsidizing vouchers for parental choice, they would have no voice in the operation of the church school or the private academies of the elite.

Nonpublic schools also deny some protections of the Constitution to their students. The "due process" provision in the Fourteenth Amendment requires procedural safeguards from arbitrary suspension or expulsion from public schools. For example, a sixth grader in a Decatur, Illinois, church school was expelled from school because her mother did not attend Sunday mass regularly. When 182 parents protested, Bishop Joseph McNicholas affirmed the suspension, replying that "Catholic education is the extension of the mission of the church. How best to fulfill this mission in individual cases rests with the pastor."[15]

There are certain implications in the proposal to provide government funds for church schools. In the United States, as in Ireland, taxpayers of all denominations and even those who do not belong to any denomination would be supporting religious, chiefly Catholic and fundamentalist Protestant, schools that are owned and managed by the bishops, priests, and other clergy. The schools would be segregated by religion, and there would be no state supervision of what is taught in the name of religion, including religious bigotry, creationism instead of evolution, and antiscientific data with respect to world population growth and sexual information. History also can be taught from a religious perspective, as can literature, by omission or reinterpretation of the contribution of other religious traditions and of such events as the Inquisition or the Church's support of fascism in Spain, Croatia, and other places.

Vouchers would eliminate protection for teachers, including salary standards or the right to depart from church requirements, such as prohibition of divorce, marriage to a person of another religion, or the use of contraception or abortion for medically necessary reasons. Teachers could be dismissed for expressing skepticism about a religious doctrine or political belief, or for exploring modern influences in philosophy, sociology, science, or other disciplines that might challenge a Catholic or fundamentalist outlook. This is because the priest or the bishop has final authority over the teacher's private life as well as his or her teaching.

The lack of government standards for teacher protection in a "school choice" system is one reason for the right-wing's favoring it, and their opposition to teacher unions. But the government ought not subsidize schools that insist on their right to use lower standards than are required in public schools.

A major issue in school vouchers is whether our educational system should move from democratic control by publicly elected school boards to a hierarchical system where a bishop or chief executive officer is in control. The advantages of democratic and constitutional control are these:

No student can be expelled and no teacher dismissed without due process of law. Accountability to the public through regular audits is not required of private schools, but is of public schools. Smith and Meier, critics of private

schools, note that "without uniform reporting requirements" by elected officials, "schools will be free to release
data on test scores, attendance, and graduation rates when
and how they see fit."[16]

Parents do not operate the school or choose the teachers
or determine the philosophy behind the teaching or any other
aspects of education. Parental choice or parental control of
education is therefore an illusion. The only choice is which
religious or other private school the parent prefers or can
afford in terms of tuition, transportation, and other costs,
which would not be met completely by government vouchers.

In short, the subsidy of religious schools by taxpayers is
support of a two- or three-tiered system of education—
public schools, religious schools, and other private
schools—with public schools consequently losing public
support because of parental choice of nonpublic schools.

Democratic control of schools insures that students are
exposed to a religious, ethnic, and class cross-section of
society with which they will have to work and engage in
civic, electoral, and other community activities in later life.
Private schools are necessarily selective in their admissions
and are often composed of elite groups of similar religious,
economic, and ethnic characteristics.

It is also to society's advantage not to have to pay taxes
to support a two-tiered school system of private and public
schools. Vouchers would support the choice not only of private academies, but Catholic, Lutheran, Christian
Reformed, Seventh-day Adventist, Jewish, Amish, Quaker,
Episcopalian, fundamentalist Christian, and evangelical
schools. This is by no means a complete list, as Muslim,

Buddhist, and even the Ku Klux Klan and other dissident white or black groups would be entitled to a share in the "choice" provided by vouchers. This nation should have learned years ago that two separate school systems, one white and the other black, were costly to operate, and the one with less political clout was an inferior system. The voucher system would be a return to this segregation.

One of the arguments for vouchers is that it would mean greater parental involvement. Most of those who use this argument do not tell us how many parents cannot be involved on a daily or even weekly basis, such as single parents without private transportation. Public schools, especially in the inner cities, exist in the context of poverty. A study by Harold Hodgkinson for the American Association of School Administrators and the National School Boards Association reveals that 15 million children are being reared by single mothers whose average family income is about $11,000. "At least 2 million children of school age have no adult supervision after school," and "on any given night from 50,000 to 200,000 children have no home. In 1988 40 percent of shelter users were families with children."[17] In addition, "eight million qualified low-income households compete for only four million low-income housing units," and many will not find "housing that provides [the] child a quiet place to study."[18] The need to earn additional income to make up the costs a voucher does not cover could even reduce parental involvement rather than increasing it.

The conclusion is that "the education system alone cannot be responsible for remedying the economic difficulties" facing these parents and their children.[19] Parental choice in education will not provide the answer, if only because the parent must usually get to work by public transportation and cannot easily get his or her children to a private school away from the neighborhood where they live or away from their workplace. And in many cases, if transportation is provided, parents would not be at home to meet the child at the end of the school day.

If we want to solve the problem of inner-city education, school choice or vouchers will be no answer. If the business elite or the administrators of religious schools want only a system of private education to exist with government funding they should say so. But if the general public wants to maintain a system of public education, then education can only be improved by equalizing educational facilities, including teacher salaries in the inner cities with those in suburbia.

Insofar as private schools seem to have higher achievement levels than inner-city schools, it is not because they are private but because of selectivity in admissions, better financial support, and the recruitment of talented students.

Quite as important is the virtual certainty that school choice legislation would be irreversible no matter how serious its shortcomings. Neither Congress nor state legislatures could withstand the political impact of religious lobbies as powerful as those who would benefit most from tax support. "School choice" and a voucher system to make it possible could be serious and far-reaching in its effects and would bolster other Vatican attempts to change American democracy.

11

VATICAN THREATS TO HEALTH CARE

T he tremendous power of the Vatican not only reaches the United States on various issues, but is seriously jeopardizing the health of many Americans, especially women. Catholics for a Free Choice reports that Catholic hospitals must follow the *Ethical and Religious Directives for Catholic Health Care Services* issued by the U.S. bishops in 1994. The pope during periodic visits by American bishops to the Vatican, whether in groups or as individuals, asks them "to report on the status of some services in their dioceses, including hospitals and other health care institutions."[1]

This has far-reaching problems for non-Catholics as well as Catholics, since as of 1998 ninety-one Catholic hospitals are located in counties and communities where there are no other hospitals or similar facilities. "Low income women who rely on hospitals for much of their health care and cannot afford to go to a private doctor or travel to distant hospitals, are affected most severely."[2] Sixty-eight of these hospitals are in counties where Catholics make up less than 25 percent of the population, and some serve counties where Catholics comprise less than 1 percent of the population. This means that the Vatican controls the health service to Jews, Protestants, Muslims, and nonreligious persons in those counties.

In 1946 when Congress passed the Hill-Burton Act to provide government funds for hospital construction, Catholic hospitals received the lion's share of the money. Between 1946 and 1960, $202.8 million (58.4 percent) went to Catholic hospitals, more than twice its proportion of the population; Protestant hospitals received $112.5 million (37.2 percent); and Jewish hospitals got $14.6 million (3.5 percent).[3]

Since many of these hospitals were built with U.S. government funds, Congress, which gave a special religious exemption to those hospitals with respect to abortion and sterilization, is ignoring the needs of American citizens in order to collaborate with the Vatican and the U.S. bishops. The serious nature of this problem is seen from the bishops' *Directives*, which specifically prohibit the prescription or dispensation of contraceptives, birth control medicines or devices, tubal ligations, vasectomies, sterilization, in vitro fertilization, and condom instruction even for patients with or at risk of contracting HIV/AIDS, as well as abortions.

It is not only hospitals that must conform to Vatican directives. Non-Catholic medical doctors who want to practice in these hospitals must agree to uphold the Catholic medical code before joining the staff of the hospital.[4]

General descriptions of Catholic medical restrictions are not adequate to describe their damage to health. For example, a woman who has been raped and wants to prevent implantation in her uterus of any fertilized egg, cannot, in a Catholic hospital, receive any medical treatment to prevent such implantation. Catholic dogma takes priority over the health of the patient, because the pope says that any preventive action after fertilization or "the moment of conception" is abortion.[5]

Actually, there is no "moment of conception." Fertilization of the ovum takes approximately one to two days. There is no test that can indicate whether or when conception has occurred, so Catholic emergency rooms could offer emergency contraception if a woman seeks it within twenty-four hours of being raped. In spite of this possibility, some hospitals have been directed by their bishops not to provide any emergency contraception in cases of rape. As a result of this ruling, in the Archdiocese of Chicago fourteen Catholic hospitals in 1992 "denied an estimated 1,004 women access to emergency contraception."[6] The only reason Congress and the administration gave these special religious privileges to government-financed Catholic hospitals is Catholic power exerted through Vatican loyalists in Congress and lobbying by the bishops.

There are numerous other illustrations of Catholic refusal to care for the health of women. Father Patrick Finney in his book *Moral Problems in Hospital Practice*, published under the imprimatur of the archbishop of St. Louis, used a question–answer form: "Q.: If it is morally certain that a pregnant mother and her unborn child will both die if the pregnancy is allowed to take its course, but at the same time the attending physician is morally certain that he can save the mother's life by removing the inviable fetus, is it lawful for him to do so? A.: No, it is not. Such a removal of the fetus would be a direct abortion."[7]

In a different Catholic question–answer column, a different issue is analyzed: "Question: My wife is sterile but wants her 'marital rights.' I have a contagious venereal disease. May I wear a prophylactic sheath? Answer: No. Even though she could not conceive and you would infect her, contraceptive intercourse is an intrinsically evil act." Professor Glanville Williams's analysis is this: "The situation [the venereal disease] makes no difference. The end sought [disease prevention] makes no difference. The act itself is wrong."[8] This is the essence not only of legalism but of Catholic sexual morality.

The increasing control of women's lives by Catholic hospitals is evident in the continuing merger of non-Catholic and Catholic hospitals. Unless non-Catholic hospitals refuse to merge without some compromise that retains the status of reproductive health services, such services are lost. That a "compromise" is possible is evident in eight cases where "public non-Catholic hospitals have continued to provide a wide range of reproductive health services despite an affiliation with or acquisition by a Catholic health system."[9] However, some Catholic health service systems are so interested in control that they do not play by any ethical rules or negotiate in good faith. After Catholic Health Services of Long Island arranged a merger with Winthrop South Nassau University Health System, the community opposed the further acquisition of Massapequa General hospital that would have resulted in the elimination of reproductive health services. The community opponents tried to block state approval of the acquisition. So the Catholic hospital bypassed the state and bought the property and buildings of Massepequa General. By becoming the landlord of the hospital, Catholic Health Services insisted on applying the *Directives* and Catholic medical restrictions, thus ending reproductive health services.[10]

Another illustration of Catholic power is the success of U.S. Catholic bishops in getting the Adolescent Family Life Act (AFLA) adopted in 1981. The act promotes periodic abstinence from sex, "natural family planning," as the only means of birth control approved by the Vatican. It discourages "teenagers from using other methods of contraception, often presenting a distorted account of the safety of those methods."[11] The law requires grant recipients to involve religious organizations in their programs, and it encourages religious groups to become grantees. At the same time the AFLA prohibits the distribution of funds to groups that provide any abortion-related services, including counseling and referral, or that subcontract with any agency that provides such services.[12] As a result the law effectively discriminates in favor of aid to Roman Catholic institutions and against most major religious organizations that do not accept Roman Catholic doctrine on abortion and contraception. The act itself, by providing for grants to any religious organization, is a violation of the letter and spirit of the federal Constitution. The restrictive wording further results in millions of dollars being made available to Roman Catholic institutions.

In the U.S. Catholic Conference brief in *Mueller* v. *Allen* (103 S. Ct. 3062, 1983) the U.S. Catholic Conference opposed the U.S. concept of separation of church and state on matters having to do with aid for Roman Catholic institutions by falsely claiming that the First Amendment did not prohibit funding religion; it was simply against preferential aid to churches. However, the Catholic bishops in the AFLA legislation demonstrated their ability to draft a law that does provide preferential aid to Catholic institutions.

The bishops are also not above using Catholic children to gain their political power in seeking to enforce Catholic dogma with respect to medicine. Waldo Zimmerman, a Roman Catholic, in his book *Condemned to Live: The Plight of the Unwanted Child*, wrote,

> The "secret weapon" in the anti-abortionists' arsenal is the millions of children in Catholic schools, their "shock troops" for staging massive demonstrations and letter-writing campaigns, Every year parochial school children look forward eagerly to January 22, when thousands of them will be treated to a free trip to Washington and other metropolitan centers for demonstrations marking the anniversary of the Supreme Court's decision on abortion.... There were as many as a thousand or two—often more—in similar demonstrations throughout the country.
>
> The January marches on Washington are staged predominantly by elementary and high school students carrying rosaries and miniature statues of the Virgin Mary. Distributed at the masses are letters and bulletins thoroughly informing parishioners about specific bills, telling them how to compose a letter to con-

gressmen or state legislators and exactly what to write. School children are offered free time and other inducements for writing such letters.

With millions of shock troops and unlimited funds, is it any wonder that the hierarchy has been able to overwhelm Congress and state legislatures with propaganda, and even to influence the Supreme Court?[13]

One of the most unethical efforts of the Catholic hierarchy in the field of health care is to exempt all Catholic medical individuals and institutions from the law, no matter what they do. The proposal placed before many state legislatures is the following: "This Act may be known and cited as the Health Care Providers' Rights of Conscience Act. . . . It is the purpose of this act to protect as a basic civil right the right of all individuals and entities to decline, to counsel, advise, pay for, provide, perform, assist, refer for or participate in providing or performing health care services that violate their religious or moral convictions."[14]

"Health care services" is defined as "any phase of patient medical care, treatment or procedure, including the following: therapy, diagnosis or prognosis, research, instruction, prescribing or administering any device, drug or medication, surgery or any other treatment rendered by health care providers or health care institution."

Such "health care services may include abortion, artificial insemination, assisted suicide, and euthanasia." This is the Vatican agenda, but some items such as cloning and human stem cell and fetal experimentation to which the

Vatican also objects have no relevance to physicians, nurses, pharmacists, and most health care individuals.

The bill is clearly designed to prevent normal medical service to women. For example, emergency contraception to a woman who has been raped would be denied, along with diagnosis and treatment if the rapist had AIDS. A woman would be denied an abortion if she had an ectopic pregnancy or uterine cancer or if her life were threatened by a dead fetus lodged crosswise in her uterus. It would even prohibit referral to another physician or hospital.

A pharmacist under this proposed law could refuse to fill certain prescriptions. This has already occurred in a decision by Walmart not to provide the drug RU-486. The bill would enable any pharmacy or individual pharmacist to refuse to fill such prescriptions or even sell condoms if that pharmacy chose not to do so. That would be comparable to a landlord or real-estate agency refusing to rent to financially qualified people for reasons of their own, such as discrimination against African Americans or Hispanic or Asian Americans.

In other words, this whole idea of legitimizing medical discrimination under the guise of conscience is really a weapon against people, chiefly women, who do not share the views of a politically powerful religious organization.

The bill would give rights of conscience to "any entity or employer that pays for any health care service or product, including HMOs . . . and insurance companies." If this bill becomes law and corporations are said by the law to have a conscience, who decides for the corporation? Can the CEO decide for the shareholders and employees, or should there be a vote? Since this is an anticontraceptives bill, does it mean that a corporation may require its workers not to use contraception, or have a child by artificial insemination?

The proposed legislation may be seen as an effort to accommodate the beliefs or decrees of a religious organization, but it results in the denial of legal and customary health care to the public. Sharon Lockhart of the Kansas chapter of the National Organization of Women presents another view:

> Nurses, physicians [and] other health care workers . . . receive licenses from the state permitting them to . . . provide services and deal in [certain] substances. . . . As such, these individuals not only are privileged by the public, but also public funds are spent in training and regulating these professions. . . . By refusing to provide legal services or products . . . these individuals violate the public trust. In essence, the monopolistic privileges granted to these persons as a group would permit the effective censoring of these legal services or products from the public if sufficient numbers of licensees refused to provide what they alone are licensed to provide. This kind of de facto censoring already can be seen . . . [when] there are no pharmacists who will provide certain drugs.[15]

The proposed act is clearly using the "conscience clause" not only to make it difficult for any woman to receive certain kinds of health care; it also forces Catholic women to accept the Vatican's program against contraceptives and abortion. An overwhelming majority of Catholic laity reject that papal position on contraceptives and on other issues. Public opinion polls reveal that if a Catholic hospital receives government or public funds, it should be required to allow its doctors to provide any legal, medically sound advice they believe is needed. Ninety-six percent of Catholic women who have ever had sex have used modern contraceptive methods. Eighty-seven percent of Catholics believe that Catholics should make up their own minds about using birth control; and another 83 percent of women believe that insurance plans that cover prescription drugs should be required to cover birth control.[16]

Americans should not confuse public opinion with the position of the Vatican or its agents, the U.S. bishops.

Throughout history, any individual or group that sought legal recognition or approval of a right of conscience was, in fact, a small minority of an essentially powerless group. One can again make a comparison with the small minority of conscientious objectors prior to World War II and before that in World War I and the Civil War. Their appeal was in their moral strength based on their willingness to suffer for their convictions, with no expectation of governmental or societal support. It was an appeal that impressed people like James Madison, Abraham Lincoln, Eleanor Roosevelt, and many members of Congress. Nevertheless, there were some objectors who went to prison for their convictions.

12

THE PAPACY, PATRIARCHY, SEXUAL MORALITY, AND CELIBACY

N o one has been more rigorous than Pope John Paul II in defending celibacy and avoiding gender equality. Except in the Eastern churches, priests who marry are forced out of their churches or in some cases laicized. Yet there are numerous priests who secretly marry or have sexual relationships with women.

Celibacy is not the same as chastity. Therefore it is possible to conform to the unmarried or celibate state and be involved sexually in secret, and thus be in technical adherence to the church rule. But this presents a serious question of ethics, not only of personal dishonesty but of the involvement of another person or persons who are also pressed into secrecy.

David Rice, a former priest, in his book *Shattered Vows*, has a chapter, "The Shadow Side of Celibacy," which details the worldwide violations of celibacy. In Pennsylvania, for example, there is "a nonprofit organization called 'Good Tidings' which helps women who have become involved with priests. The leader of the organization says she has over seven hundred women on her books."[1]

An active priest wrote in the Franciscan magazine *St. Anthony's Messenger* in 1986 that "mandatory celibacy has become the millstone around the neck of the priesthood and is threatening to destroy it." David Rice summarized the priest's article as follows: "The law of celibacy is routinely flouted by many priests; some of them have secretly married and pass off their wives as live-in housekeepers in the rectory. Others . . . have taken lovers. The law has also led to 'rampant psychosexual problems' including a huge increase in reported cases of child molestation and a 'noticeable increase in the number of gay seminarians' at Catholic divinity schools."[2]

Catholic theologian Richard McBrien, in an article in the June 19, 1987, *Commonweal,* suggests that the priesthood may be "attractive to certain people precisely because it excludes marriage. To put it plainly, as long as the Church requires celibacy for the ordained priesthood, the priesthood will always pose a particular attraction for gay men who are otherwise not drawn to ministry." In effect it provides them "occupational respectability and freedom from social suspicion."

Rice said "compulsory celibacy does not work." The result is "thousands of men leading double lives, thousands of women leading destroyed lives, thousands of children spurned by their ordained fathers, to say nothing of . . . the psychiatric cases, the alcoholics and the workaholics."[3]

Rice added, "Yes, our men in the Vatican know."[4]

The Vatican's rough response is that if priests resign or

are married or exposed, they lose their pensions, insurance, and may be excommunicated.

Why does the Vatican continue to insist on celibacy? According to Rice, celibacy is a "control factor *par excellence*. Bachelors are simply easier to manage. There is no family to care for; there is no wife to counsel disobedience or to stiffen resolve; there is no danger of nepotism or of children inheriting church property."[5]

Actually, there is in some places nearly open disregard for the celibacy rule. In some parts of the world more than half of all priests live with women: 80 percent in Peru; between 60 and 70 percent in Brazil; over 50 percent in the Philippines; and parts of Africa may approach even higher rates.[6] In fact, in March 2001 the *National Catholic Reporter* reported the use of nuns for sex by priests and higher clergy, because the nuns do not pose the risk of HIV as do other women in some AIDS-racked countries of Africa. In at least one situation the young nun became pregnant and an abortion was arranged.[7]

In 2002 the church faced an avalanche of accusations of priests and several bishops for pedophilia and child abuse. It was not confined to the United States: Publicity here led to similar revelations in other countries. Analysis of the crisis included factors such as the authoritarian control by the bishops, including a massive effort of the hierarchy to conceal such conduct, paying millions of dollars to do so. Another factor was said to be the shortage of priests and a resulting lack of screening to eliminate any man with tendencies to pedophilia. A third factor was the obvious one—the rule of celibacy prohibiting marriage. One writer commenting on the crisis in the April 19, 2002, *New York Times* said, "Liberals, and many experts who have treated sexually abusive priests, say the abuse of the crisis is the church's lack of candor about sexuality and the strictures about priestly celibacy. The problem arises, they say, when sexually stunted and inexperienced young men are recruited into an institution in which sex is taboo, incubated in the all-male hothouse called a seminary, and then are deposited into a lonely occupation where a good part of their human connection is with young boys."[8]

The American cardinals were summoned to Rome for two days' discussion with the pope April 23–24. The *New York Times* of April 20 reported that Cardinal Roger Mahoney of Los Angeles "has publicly commented that he felt the church ought to debate allowing priests to be married. . . . In fact, he said . . . he would push to use this crisis to make the church's decision-making more transparent and to create a church that is more humble."[9]

Nevertheless, in a statement issued by the American cardinals at the end of the meeting in Rome, "the church leaders declared that 'a link between pedophilia and celibacy cannot scientifically be maintained,' and the group, as expected, reaffirmed priestly celibacy."[10]

There is serious inconsistency in the compulsory celibacy rule. In the Eastern Catholic Church priests have always been free to marry. And in the United States and England, a number of married Protestant clergy who oppose women ministers and bishops in their churches convert to Catholicism and are accepted as ordained priests in the Roman Church, which is opposed to the ordination of women.

These issues are not unrelated. One plausible and perhaps the dominant reason for male celibacy, and for the acceptance of married Protestant clergy who do not want to serve with women, is patriarchy. The Roman Catholic Church will not risk even the slightest opening of the door to equality of women, lest men eventually lose control at all levels of the church. What does the church lose in continuing the celibacy rule? One thing is the obvious disconnect in the fact of a celibate priest extolling the sanctity of marriage and the family. Moreover, if he is genuinely not living with a woman, the parish priest is deprived of the personal experience of both affection and human sympathy, and is therefore less helpful in understanding and aiding in the joys and sorrows of the families in his parish.

Rice indicates that modern priests are keenly aware of this deficiency, and in the light of new respect for women, see the need for partnership in both ministry and in life. There is the recognition and celebration of sexuality, and a renewal of the role of individual conscience against the strictures of compelled behavior. What does that mean in terms of numbers? By the date of Rice's book (1990) there were more than 100,000 priests who had left their ministry, which is "close to a quarter of all the active priests in the world." According to sociologist Richard Schoenherr, 42 percent of all American priests leave the priesthood within twenty-five years of ordination.[11]

In 1966, "there were 42,767 seminarians in the United States." By 1996, "while the Catholic population increased by more than 50 percent," they numbered "only slightly over 6,000." Because of the decreasing number of new priests each year, "the average age of priests . . . is 65 years."[12]

Does this mean that non-Catholics should rejoice at this massive exodus? Not at all. It has been a personal and institutional tragedy. If the Roman Catholic Church is nudged by its reformers who still love the church into treating marriage of both clergy and laity as a great institution, women as equals to men, sexuality as good, and conscience as superior to patriarchal dogma, the world will be a better place. There will be greater respect for family planning and birth control as well as concern for overpopulation and the environment. In short, non-Catholics should welcome the Catholic reform movement and unofficial agencies within the Catholic church, such as Catholics for a Free Choice. Likewise, Protestant church leaders engaged in ecumenical dialogue with their Catholic counterparts should make it clear that ecumenism must include major reforms and not be dependent on minor theological concessions.

13

THE FUTURE OF AMERICAN DEMOCRACY

In view of the efforts by the Vatican and the American bishops to control the policies of federal and state governments, what does the future portend for American democracy?

One scenario is that enough politicians will be prepared to oppose the Catholic bishops and their right-wing Protestant allies on the crucial issues of abortion, birth control, the rights of women, aid to church schools, and an independent judiciary, so that they will again and again be unable to achieve their goals. That scenario depends on many imponderables, such as whether moderate Republicans are able to withstand the effort to achieve a complete takeover of their party by right-wing Catholic and Protestant groups; whether future presidents will be free from the illusion that they must do what the bishops want on these issues; and whether progressive Catholics, Protestants, Jews, and others can organize to prevent the adoption of all or most of the Vatican agenda.

One key factor in this scenario is whether the bishops can succeed in overcoming progressive Catholics who have not only been "Americanized" in their belief in democratic government, but who have a different view of their church. Archbishop Rembert G. Weakland of Milwaukee warned American Catholics, in an article in the October 18, 1986, Jesuit weekly *America*, to beware of "integralism," which in the past "sought a complete or integral Catholicism in the political realm [and] demanded the perfect coalescence of Christian morality with the legal realm of the state and, thus, the suppression of all error. No concept of separation of church and state was considered orthodox. Error has no rights, they said; and, since the Catholic Church is considered the source of all truth, its doctrine alone should dominate in political affairs."[1]

The policy of integralism "spawned Catholic political parties, Catholic labor unions, organizations of Catholic industrialists, and other such associations," wrote Penny Lernoux.[2] "The most difficult question posed to the Church today by the American political process is precisely that of compromise, a solution inevitable in a pluralistic society," said Archbishop Weakland. "The whole theory of integralism returns to haunt us at this point of the discussion. Vatican II rejected integralism, but it did not indicate where compromise must stop."[3]

The concept of "integralism" and "no compromise" have become evident not only with respect to political and governmental officials, but also at other levels. Archbishop Pilarcyzk of Cincinnati, speaking about a Roman Catholic employee of Planned Parenthood and her work as "manifest moral evil," said, "Promoting, managing, or operating abortion facilities are examples of such conduct, and Catholics who obstinately persist in these activities, while perhaps not formally excommunicated, should not consider themselves properly disposed to participate in the church's banquet of unity by receiving Holy Communion."[4] Earlier the *Washington Post* of September 15, 1986, reported that "Church authorities in two separate dioceses this year have moved against girls whose mothers were active in Planned Parenthood; in one case excommunicating the mother, and in the other, forcing the youngster out of parochial school." The *Post* also quoted Washington Archbishop James A. Hickey as saying "there is no right to public dissent" within the Church.[5]

Integralism is also manifest in a fidelity or loyalty oath, instituted in 1989, which is taken with hands on a Bible. It requires "teachers in any universities whatsoever who teach disciplines which deal with faith or morals" as well as pastors, deacons, seminary rectors, rectors of universities, and diocesan officials to adhere to the rule of the Vatican.[6] The oath requires obedience to whatever may issue in the future from the Vatican or the bishops, as well as what has already been proclaimed. One of the sentences of the oath says "I adhere with religious submission of will and intellect to the teachings which either the Roman pontiff or the College of Bishops enunciate when they exercise the authentic magisterium, even if they proclaim those teachings in an act that is not definitive."[7]

Over against this policy of "integralism" is the growth of a largely unorganized number of progressive Catholics who do not permit the bishops to determine their politics or their actions. For example, on the crucial issue of abortion, public opinion polls taken in the mid-1990s reveal that most Catholics are pro-choice, and as voters do not follow the bishops. "Catholics make up their own minds," according to Catholics for a Free Choice, with headquarters in Washington, D.C. That organization indicated that, as of 1995, the number of Catholics in the United States is about 60 million, but this count includes everyone baptized and does not reflect recent losses or lapsed members. The official figures show that Catholics comprise 22 percent of the total U.S. population. Catholics made up 29 percent of voters in the U.S. House races on election day 1994. Thirteen percent of Catholics say abortion can never be a morally acceptable choice. And seventy percent say Catholics can vote in good conscience for candidates who support legal abortion.[8]

Further evidence for Catholic opinion is included in the following polls:[9]

• *Time*/CNN nationwide poll of 1,000 adults, September 27–28, 1994, subsample of 500 Catholics: "A full 82 percent of U.S. Catholics say abortion should be legal either under certain circumstances or without restrictions. This is close to the figure for all Americans, 87 percent. Among Catholics 39 percent say a woman should be able to get an abortion if she decides she wants one, no matter what the reason. Another 43 percent say abortion should be legal under certain circumstances, such as when a woman's health is endangered or when a pregnancy results from rape. Only 15 percent of Catholics agree with the bishops' position that abortion should be illegal in all circumstances."

• Gallup Survey for Catholics Speak Out, of 802

Catholics, May 4-9 1992: "84 percent of Catholics and 84 percent of all Americans said abortion should be legal in some or all circumstances. Only 13 percent of Catholics agreed with the bishops that abortion should be illegal in all circumstances." Also, "70 percent of Catholics agree or strongly agree with the statement that Catholics can, in good conscience, vote for political candidates who support legal abortions."

• *Los Angeles Times* poll of 1,374 adults and 1,149 registered voters, April 13–16, 1996, Catholic subsample 418: "66 percent of all Catholics say President Clinton's veto of the late-term abortion bill in April 1996 will make no difference in their choice between Clinton and Dole in the presidential elections or will make them more likely to vote for Clinton. Just after Clinton vetoed the late term abortion bill, Catholics preferred Clinton over Dole by 58 percent to 33 percent."

• *New York Times*/CBS News poll of 1,536 adults nationwide, subsample of 423 Catholics, September 18–22, 1995: "Just before the 1995 papal visit, 75 percent of U.S. Catholics said that knowing the pope's position on a social or political issue would not influence their positions on the issue. Only 16 percent said they would be more likely to support the pope's position."

• ABC/*Washington Post* poll of 1,530 adults, September 28 to October 1, 1995: "67 percent of Catholics believe a woman who has an abortion for reasons other than to save her life can still be a good Catholic."

• Survey by Alan Guttmacher Institute of 9,480 women obtaining abortions in 1987: "Catholic women are as likely as all other U.S. women to have abortions, and 36 percent more likely than Protestant women."

• Survey by Alan Guttmacher Institute of 1,900 women obtaining abortions in 1987–1988: "When asked about their reasons for having abortions, Catholics are 8 percent more likely than those of different religious beliefs to say they do not want others to find out about their sexual activity or pregnancy."

• *U.S. News & World Report* survey of 1,000 American adults, subsample of 493 Catholics, September 23–24, 1995: "82 percent of Catholics disapproved or strongly disapproved of the statement that using artificial birth control, such as condoms or birth control pills, is morally wrong."

• *Time*/CNN nationwide poll of 1,000 adults and subsample of 500 Catholics, September 27–28, 1995: "76 percent of Catholics disagreed with the statement that using artificial means of birth control is wrong."

Most progressive Catholics are not organized as a political group. However, there are approximately ten unofficial Catholic groups who have joined in a National Task Force of "We Are the Church" Coalition to seek major Church reforms, such as the following:

1. A loving church where the equality of all the faithful is respected, the gulf between clergy and laity is bridged, and the People of God participate in the process of selecting their bishops and pastors.
2. A church with equal rights for women, where women are full participants in all official decision making and are welcomed in all ministries.
3. A church where priests may choose either a celibate or noncelibate way of life.
4. A church which affirms the goodness of sexuality, the

primacy of conscience in deciding issues of sexual morality (e. g., birth control), the human rights of all persons regardless of sexual orientation, and the importance and urgency of issues other than sexual morality (e.g., peace and nonviolence, social justice, preservation of the environment).

5. A church which affirms people rather than condemns them, respects primacy of conscience in all moral decision making, embraces and welcomes those who are divorced and remarried, married priests, theologians and others who exercise freedom of speech.[10]

This reform effort may have some political overtones, but it has not included in its list of reforms a recognition of a separation of church and state, or defense of the public schools, or other items essential to the preservation of American democracy. It does not, of course, have access through official channels to millions of Catholics who might reject integralism. Nevertheless, it is a welcome development on the American religious scene.

A second scenario concerning the future of the Roman Catholic Church is one in which the bishops are able to maintain not only their image and official influence, but also their recent leadership of non-Catholic right-wing groups which include the Mormons, a large number of Southern Baptists, and a host of far-right organizations such as the Christian Coalition, Focus on the Family, Coral Ridge Ministries, Family Research Council, Concerned Women for America, and the Eagle Forum. All of these groups and others too numerous to mention here have accepted the bishops' political agenda without accepting all of Vatican theology. This scenario presupposes the continued, largely unrestricted growth of Catholic immigrants from Latin America, the success of the educational efforts of bishops and priests in advancing integralism, and the continuing silence or lack of criticism of the bishops' agenda in the press. It also includes the silence of mainstream Protestant leaders held captive by discussions of ecumenical unity and by fear of reviving charges of anti-Catholic bigotry, despite the fact that bigotry in modern America is almost entirely directed at minority religions rather than powerful or majority groups.

This second scenario also presupposes the bishops' success in sustaining the illusion that they speak politically for, or are able to influence the votes of, Catholic citizens.

There is no other country that offers a perfect illustration of what the United States would look like under increased Vatican influence or control. There is, however, value in examining the situation in Ireland where the government, without actually making the Catholic Church an official religion, is very responsive to the Irish bishops. It also has a state-supported segregated school system in which the very few Protestant schools are also subsidized. The headquarters of the Catholic bishops at Maynooth is sometimes referred to as the "Purple Parliament" because of its influence on the state Parliament in Dublin.

The Irish government has no separation of church and state, forbids abortion, and for years has forbidden divorce and remarriage of divorced persons. Although in some respects it has a free press, the press is aware that it cannot criticize the dominant religious-political influence.

Obviously there would be differences, but in the United States, once the bishops and their allies became dominant, legislative and judicial interpretations would reflect the morals, customs, educational values, and other demands of the Vatican. For example, in 1983 the U.S. Catholic Conference, that is, the bishops, filed an amicus brief, in the Supreme Court with respect to *Mueller* v. *Allen* in an effort to obtain a Court ruling that the First Amendment clause prohibiting an establishment of religion really prohibits only preferential aid to churches and not to churches as such.[11]

The First Amendment says there shall be no establishment of religion. The word "establishment" has two meanings. One is an institution or organization of religion. Obviously the amendment was not prohibiting religious groups organizing their own establishment(s). What it does refer to is no government sponsorship including no financial support of any religious organization.

The bishops claimed that the First Amendment does not specifically forbid aid to churches, only the establishment of a single, government-supported religion. This is not the case. When the First Amendment was adopted, there were six states that had comprehensive or multiple establishments. That is, aid was provided to all churches on a non-preferential basis. It was this practice that the framers of the First Amendment confronted and what they understood constituted an establishment of religion.

In a situation in which the Church is the established religion, the church would be dominant. For example, in the United States territory of Guam, which is subject to U.S. law, the legislature adopted a law against abortion, specifying that anyone who provides an abortion can be charged with a felony, anyone who has an abortion commits a crime, and anyone who merely gives information about abortion is liable for a $1,000 fine or a year in jail. While the bill was before the legislature, all but one of whose twenty-one members were Roman Catholics, Archbishop Anthony Apuron, in a televised statement, threatened to excommunicate any legislator who voted against the bill.[12]

A courageous Catholic woman, Frances Kissling, president of the U.S.-based Catholics for a Free Choice, in an address in the British House of Lords to an All Party Parliamentary Group on Population, Development, and Reproductive Health, spoke of another country where the Church has exerted its power:

> Take, for example, the case of Poland, perhaps the most poignant illustration of the effect that the institutional church can have on women's lives and family life. Poles who viewed the church as a democratizing force now say, "We have exchanged a red dictatorship for a black one"—meaning the church. Abortion has become illegal while contraceptives are still less than universally available. In Poland, women are asked to have more childen at the same time that day care is eliminated with church approval. The Pope has started a non-governmental organization called Pharmacists for Life. Those pharmacists who are opposed to contraception go into pharmacies around the country, buy up what meager stocks of contraceptives are available, and destroy them. In this country, they

organize to oppose the availability of emergency contraception and services for young people.[13]

She then noted that in the United States,

Catholic Relief Services, which has an annual budget of $290 million, received about 77 percent of its resources from the U.S. government. Is this a Catholic agency or a government agency? Catholic agencies are recognized for the quality of their assistance. . . . However, when it comes to the question of women's rights, especially reproductive health, these agencies are simply not able to implement government policies which require that aid recipients have access to family planning and the human right to make their own decisions about the number and spacing of their children."[14]

There are numerous other illustrations of hidden federal and state governmental aid to Catholic agencies which follow Church policies, such as the funding authorized under the U.S. "Adolescent Family Life Act" discussed previously. The Catholic bishops are even trying to influence the judiciary and lawyers associations through the "Red Mass." The bishops invite members of the Supreme Court and other courts and attorneys to these events, where they mingle politics and religion. For example, in 1989 with Supreme Court justices in attendance, Philadelphia's Archbishop Anthony J. Bevilaqua, now a cardinal, presented arguments against separation of church and state. In 1995 with the president, Supreme Court justices, and other government officials present, Cardinal James Hickey pressed for a deemphasis on the Establishment Clause, and in New York Cardinal John O'Connor warned Catholic judges and lawyers of their obligation to put [the Church's] spiritual teaching above civil law. All over the country, bishops invite legislators and judges to hear their plea to put Catholic moral law ahead of civil law.[15]

It is quite possible to develop a scenario in which the United States under increasing Vatican influence would at some point resemble a combination of Poland, Ireland, and even countries where there is an official concordat with the Vatican.

Everything depends on whether the American people are willing to acquiesce in the step-by-step erosion of their liberties, in addition to the step-by-step action of Congress and state legislators to appropriate their tax money for use by powerful religious agencies. No people can rely on the Vatican or any other power group to restrain itself.

*   *   *   *   *

Any concluding postscript or appraisal of the Roman Catholic Church must recognize that it has many facets and meets many needs. One of its admirable features is its many members who want it to be a servant church rather than a power church seeking control not only over its own members but also nonmembers by seeking control of the government in nations where they reside. There is a Catholic reform movement in various nations that believes patriarchal control and subordination of women should yield to a recognition of sexual or gender equality and to respect for the sacrament of marriage, at present the only sacrament from which its priests are barred.

The Catholic reform movement seeks respect for individual conscience and reverence for all life, including the lives of women threatened by a dangerous pregnancy. It is exceedingly difficult for elderly celibate men in the Vatican to understand the health concerns a man has for his wife or the importance of her health to already-existing children.

There are many in and out of the Church who object to universal rules for which there are no exceptions, known as legalism. Some of these rules deny to men and women the use of protective barriers in sexual relations to prevent the spread of AIDS or other diseases.

It is a matter of concern to many non-Catholics that their differing religious traditions and their ethical values are not respected when the Vatican seeks to impose upon them laws or rules prescribed by the Vatican. It is also a matter of concern that the Vatican talks about an end to poverty, war, and other social problems but does nothing to deal with them while investing its tremendous resources and influence on matters related to sex.

Finally, there are millions of Catholics and non-Catholics who want the Church at its every level to reject totalitarian control by any government and to support a democracy of the people, by the people, and for the people.

NOTES

Chapter 2.

1. *Summa Iuris Publici Ecclesiastici ad normram Codicis Iuris Canonici et recentiorum S. Sedis Documentorum concinnata,* Auctore Felice Cappello S.J. 2d ed. (Rome, 1928).

Chapter 3.

1. Quoted in Aaron Abell, *The Urban Impact on American Protestantism, 1865–1900* (Cambridge, Mass.: Harvard University Press, 1943), p. 63

Chapter 5.

1. John A. Ryan and Francis J. Boland, *Catholic Principles of Politics* (New York: Macmillan, 1960), p. 313–14.
2. *New York Times,* June 14, 1965.
3. *National Catholic Reporter,* October 11, 1985.

4. Penny Lernoux, *People of God* (New York: Viking/Penguin, 1989), p. 206.

5. Ibid., p. 207.

6. Ibid., p. 208.

7. Emilio Mignone, *The Complicity of Church and Dictatorship in Argentina* (Maryknoll, N.Y.: Orbis Books, 1988), pp. 49, 97.

8. Jean-Guy Villaincourt, *Papal Power: A Study of Vatican Control over Lay Catholic Elites* (Berkeley: University of California Press, 1980), p. 272.

9. "The Vatican Connection," *The Humanist*, November–December 1996.

10. *A New Rite: Conservative Catholic Organizations and Their Allies* (Washington, D.C.: Catholics for a Free Choice, 1994), p. 14.

11. Joseph Conn, *Church and State*, April 1993.

12. Timothy Byrnes, *Catholic Bishops in American Politics* (Princeton, N.J.: Princeton University Press, 1991), p. 58.

13. *Pastoral Plan for Pro-Life Activities*, November 20, 1975 (Washington, D.C.: National Council of Catholic Bishops); see also Byrnes, *Catholic Bishops*, p. 59.

14. *Pastoral Plan.*

15. Connie Paige, *The Right-to-Lifers* (New York: Summit Books, 1983), p. 155.

16. Ibid., p. 166.

17. Richard A. Viguerie, *The New Right: We're Ready to Lead* (Falls Church, Va.: Viguerie Company, 1980), p. 56.

18. Ralph Reed, *Active Faith* (New York: Free Press, 1996), p. 216.

19. Ibid.

20. *A New Rite*, p. 6.

21. Ibid.

22. *National Catholic Reporter*, December 22, 1996.

23. *National Catholic Reporter*, July 31, 1992.

24. *Evangelium Vitae*; see also "Pope Asks Disobedience to U.S. Law," *The Churchman/Human Quest*, March–April 1996.

25. *New York Times*, May 4, 1996.

26. *New York Times*, June 26, 1996.

27. *New York Times*, July 19, 1996.

28. *National Catholic Reporter*, July 26, 1996, pp. 9, 10.

29. *New York Times*, June 24, 1996.

30. *The Wanderer*, April 23, 1992, p. 1.

31. *A New Rite*, p. 9.

32. United Nations Fund for Population Activities, 1991 Population Issues briefing kit.

33. Hal Kane, *World Watch*, January–February 1995.

Chapter 6.

1. *Our Sunday Visitor*, 1993, p. 239.

2. *Free Thought Today*, October 1993, p. 4.

3. See Stephen Mumford, *The Life and Death of NSSM 200* (Research Triangle Park, N.C.: Center for Research on Population and Security, 1996), pp. 259–75.

4. *The Wanderer*, July 18, 1996, p. 3.

5. *The Catalyst*, July–August 1994, p. 3.

6. *The Catalyst*, December 1995, p. 3.

7. *The Catalyst*, July–August 1994, p. 3.

8. Mumford, *The Life and Death of NSSM 200*, p. 286.

9. *The Catalyst*, March 1995, p. 11.

10. *The Catalyst*, November 1995, p. 1.

11. *The Catalyst*, May 1995, p. 1.

12. *The Catalyst*, September 1995, p. 5.

13. Mumford, *The Life and Death of NSSM 200*, p. 293.

14. *The Catalyst*, March 1995, p. 11.

15. Mumford, *The Life and Death of NSSM 200*, p. 298.

16. Ibid., p. 299.

17. Associated Press, October 5, 1997.

Chapter 7.

1. A. B. Hasler, *How The Pope Became Infallible* (New York: Doubleday, 1981), p. 14.

2. Hans Küng, *Infallibility? An Inquiry* (Garden City, N.Y.: Image Books, Doubleday, 1972), p. 85.

3. Küng, statement in *National Catholic Reporter*, October 11, 1985.

4. Stephen Mumford, *The Life and Death of NSSM 200*, (Research Triangle Park, N.C.: Center for Research of Population and Security, 1996), p. 124.

5. Hasler, *How the Pope Became Infallible*, p. 126.

6. *Humanae Vitae*, 1968; see also the Vatican "Instruction on Respect for Human Life in its Origin and on the Dignity of Procreation," 1987.

7. Michael Schwartz, *Persistent Prejudice: Anti-Catholicism in America* (Huntington, Ind.: Our Sunday Visitor Press, 1984), p. 132.

8. National Conference of Catholic Bishops, "Pastoral Plan for Pro-Life Activities," November 2, 1975.

9. Emilio F. Mignone, *Witness to the Truth: The Complicity of Church and Dictatorship in Argentina* (Maryknoll, N.Y.: Orbis Books, 1988).

10. Editorial, *New York Times*, September 27, 1988.

11. Cited in Hasler, *How the Pope Became Infallible*, p. 25.

12. Cited in Mumford, *The Life and Death of NSSM 200*, p. 215.

Chapter 8.

1. Wayne Barrett, *Village Voice* December 25, 1984.
2. Ibid.
3. Ibid.
4. Ibid.
5. Ibid.
6. Ibid.
7. Ibid.
8. Anna Maria Escurra, *The Vatican and the Reagan Administration* (New York: Circus Publications, 1986), p. 128.
9. Timothy Byrnes, *Catholic Bishops in American Politics* (Princeton, N.J.: Princeton University Press, 1991), p. 73.
10. Ibid., p. 74.
11. Ibid.
12. "Roman Catholic Church Sets U.S. Policy," *The Churchman/Human Quest*, March–April 1992. The full text of the Ravenholt address is available from the Center for Research on Population and Security, P.O. Box 1307, Research Triangle Park, N.C. 27709.
13. Ibid.
14. Ibid.
15. Ibid.
16. Byrnes, *Catholic Bishops in American Politics*, p. 76.
17. *National Catholic Reporter*, December 29, 1989.
18. Ibid.
19. Stephen Mumford, *The Life and Death of NSSM 200*, (Research Triangle Park, N.C.: Center for Research of Population and Security, 1996), p. 355.
20. *New York Times*, August 6, 1992.
21. Mumford, *The Life and Death of NSSM 200*, p. 164.
22. *New York Times*, May 28, 1992.

23. Sierra Club release, "Misleading America on Family Values and Population: The Two Faces of George Bush," July 9, 1992.

24. Ibid.

25. *Kansas City Star*, September 13, 1996.

26. *National Catholic Reporter*, May 31, 1996.

27. Words by Battle are from the *Catechism of the Catholic Church*; Canon 747, Sec. 7 of the *Code of Canon Law*; and Vatican II, "Gaudium et Spes," Pastoral Constitution on the Church in the Modern World.

28. *New York Times*, September 5, 1994.

29. *Kansas City Star*, May 20, 1997.

30. *Kansas City Star*, May 16, 1997.

Chapter 9.

1. A. B. Hasler, *How the Pope Became Infallible* (New York: Doubleday, 1981), pp. 81 ff.

2. Paul Blanshard, *American Freedom and Catholic Power*, 2d ed. (Boston: Beacon Press, 1958), p. 36.

3. Williston Walker, *A History of the Christian Church* (New York: Charles Scribner's Sons, 1943), pp. 131–35.

4. Ibid., pp. 240–44.

5. "Innocent III," *Collier's Encyclopedia*, vol. 13, New York: Crowell-Collier, 1967, p. 30.

6. Ibid., vol. 13, p. 32.

7. Ibid., vol. 13, p. 31.

8. Ibid., vol. 13, p. 30.

9. Paul Blanshard, *American Freedom and Catholic Power*, (Boston: Beacon Press, 1960), pp. 279, 280.

10. Ibid., p. 284, 285.

11. Ibid., p. 288.

12. Ibid., pp. 287, 289.

13. *National Catholic Reporter,* October 10, 1997.

14. James Carroll, "The Silence," *New Yorker,* April 7, 1997.

15. Ibid.

16. United Nations Fund for Population Activities, 1991 briefing kit.

17. *New Yorker,* June 1, 1992.

18. *New York Times,* May 28, 1992.

19. Ibid.

20. William K. Stevens, *New York Times,* May 5, 1992.

21. Quoted in the *Washington Post,* May 14, 1992.

22. Ibid.

23. Anthony Lewis, *New York Times,* July 10, 1992.

24. William K. Stevens, *New York Times,* May 5, 1992.

25. Ibid.

26. *All Things Considered,* National Public Radio, October 22, 1997.

27. *National Catholic Reporter,* August 29, 1997.

28. John S. Spong, "Roman Catholic-Anglican Ecumenical Union: A Cause I Can No Longer Support," *Virginia Quarterly Review,* spring 1992.

Chapter 10.

1. *U.S. News & World Report,* October 25, 1957.

2. Vatican Council II, *The Conciliar and Post Conciliar Documents,* Austin Flannery, O.P., gen. ed. (Northport, N.Y.: Costello Publishing Co., 1977), p. 731.

3. William W. Cooley, *School Choice or School Reform,* Pennsylvania Educational Policy Studies, no. 12 (Pittsburgh: University of Pittsburgh, Learning Research and Development Center, 1991; also cited in David C. Berliner and Bruce J. Biddle, *The*

Manufactured Crisis (Reading, Mass.: Addison-Wesley Publishing Company, 1995), p. 177.

4. Albert J. Menendez, unpublished study for Americans for Religious Liberty, gathered from 1990 U.S. Census data and Glenmary Research Center Publications, *Churches and Church Membership in the United States.*

5. Ibid.

6. Ibid.

7. Berliner and Biddle, *The Manufactured Crisis,* pp. 149–51.

8. *Money,* October 1994.

9. Arnold Fege, "Private School Vouchers: Separate and Unequal" in *Why We Still Need Public Schools,* Art Must Jr. (Buffalo, N.Y.: Prometheus Books, 1992), pp. 226–27.

10. *New York Times,* June 9, 1995.

11. James Michael Lee, ed., *Catholic Education in the Western World* (South Bend, Ind.: University of Notre Dame, 1967), p. 217.

12. Thomas J. Reese, *Archbishop: Inside the Power Structure* (New York: Harper and Row, 1989), p. 273.

13. *School Choice* (Princeton, N.J.: Carnegie Foundation for the Advancement of Teaching, 1992), p. 24–25.

14. Donald E. Frey, cited in *Christian Social Action,* September 1993, p. 15; see also Frey, "What If Government Subsidies for Private Schools Are Legislated?" in Must, *Why We Still Need Public Schools,* p. 198.

15. Cited in "R. C. Campaign for Parochial Expansion," *The Churchman/Human Quest,* May–June 1991.

16. Kevin B. Smith and Kenneth J. Meier, *The Case against School Choice* (Armonk, N.Y.: M. E. Sharpe, 1995), p. 38.

17. Henry Hodgkinson, *Beyond the Schools* (Arlington, Va.: American Association of School Administrators).

18. Ibid.
19. Ibid.

Chapter 11.

1. *Catholic Health Care Restrictions May Be Hazardous to Your Health* (Washington, D.C.: Catholics for a Free Choice, 1999), p. 6.
2. Ibid., p. 6.
3. Lawrence Lader, *Politics, Power, and the Church* (New York: Macmillan, 1987), p. 76.
4. Ibid.
5. Ibid., p. 78.
6. *Catholic Health Restrictions*, pp. 8, 9.
7. Patrick Finney, *Moral Problems in Hospital Practice* (St. Louis, London: B. Herder Book Co., 1935)
8. Lader, *Politics, Power, and the Church*, p. 77.
9. *Catholic Health Restrictions*, p. 5.
10. Ibid.
11. Patricia Donovan, "The Adolescent Family Life Act and the Promotion of Religious Doctrine," *Family Planning Perspectives* 16, no. 5 (September/October 1984): 222.
12. Ibid.
13. Waldo Zimmerman, *Condemned to Live: The Plight of the Unwanted Child* (Memphis, Tenn.: Vida Press, 1981), pp. 32, 33.
14. Text of Kansas House bill 2491, 2001.
15. Testimony before Kansas House legislature committee on House bill 2491, March 2001.
16. Catholics for a Free Choice *Everything You Always Wanted to Know about the Catholic Vote*; for more current information consult CWFAC, 1436 U. Street, NW., Suite 301, Washington, D.C., 20009-3997.

Chapter 12.

1. David Rice, *Shattered Vows: Priests Who Leave* (New York, William Morrow, 1990), p. 116.
2. Ibid., p. 117.
3. Ibid., pp. 126, 127.
4. Ibid., p. 128.
5. Ibid., p. 135.
6. Ibid., p. 120.
7. *National Catholic Reporter*, March 10, 2001.
8. Laurie Goodstein, "Homosexuality in Priesthood Is Under Increasing Scrutiny," *New York Times*, April 19, 2002.
9. Melinda Hennenbeger and James Sterngold, "Vatican Meeting on Abuse Issue Is Set to Confront Thorny Topics," *New York Times*, April 19, 2002.
10. Julie Lieblich, "Abuse Policy Is Promised," *New York Times*, April 25, 2002.
11. Richard A. Schoenherr, *Power and Authority in Organized Religion*, quoted in Rice, *Shattered Vows*, p. 11.
12. "1992 Status Report/Vocations," Catholic Church Extension Society, Chicago, cited in Stephen Mumford, *The Life and Death of NSSM 200* (Research Triangle Park, N.C.: Center for Research on Population and Security, 1996), p. 204.

Chapter 13.

1. Quoted in Penny Lernoux, *People of God* (New York: Viking/Penguin, 1989), p. 255.
2. National Catholic Reporter, p. 256.
3. Ibid.
4. *Kansas City Star*, March 10, 1990.
5. *Washington Post*, September 15, 1986.

6. *National Catholic Reporter*, March 17, 1989; June 30, 1989.

7. *National Catholic Reporter*, March 17, 1989.

8. Poll conducted in 1995 by Catholics for a Free Choice, 1436 U. Street NW, Suite 301, Washington, D.C., 20009. See also *Everything You Always Wanted to Know about the Catholic Vote* (Washington, D.C.: Catholics for a Free Choice, 1996).

9. Ibid.

10. *National Catholic Reporter*, May 31, 1996, p. 5.

11. John Swomley, *Religious Liberty and the Secular State* (Buffalo, N.Y.: Prometheus Books, 1987), pp. 38, 50, 132.

12. Ellen Goodman, *Boston Globe*, March 22, 1990; *New York Times*, March 21, 1990.

13. Frances Kissling, *The Vatican and Politics of Reproductive Health* (Washington, D.C.: Catholics for a Free Choice), p. 7.

14. Ibid., pp. 7, 8.

15. Albert J. Menendez, *The Red Mass: A Fusion of Religion and Politics* (Silver Spring, Md.: Americans for Religious Liberty, 1997).

INDEX